Drunken Barnaby's four journeys to the north of England. In Latin and English metre. ... Together with Bessy Bell. The fourth edition.

Richard Brathwait

PRINT EDITIONS

Eighteenth Century
Collections Online
Print Editions

Gale ECCO Print Editions

Relive history with *Eighteenth Century Collections Online*, now available in print for the independent historian and collector. This series includes the most significant English-language and foreign-language works printed in Great Britain during the eighteenth century, and is organized in seven different subject areas including literature and language; medicine, science, and technology; and religion and philosophy. The collection also includes thousands of important works from the Americas.

The eighteenth century has been called "The Age of Enlightenment." It was a period of rapid advance in print culture and publishing, in world exploration, and in the rapid growth of science and technology – all of which had a profound impact on the political and cultural landscape. At the end of the century the American Revolution, French Revolution and Industrial Revolution, perhaps three of the most significant events in modern history, set in motion developments that eventually dominated world political, economic, and social life.

In a groundbreaking effort, Gale initiated a revolution of its own: digitization of epic proportions to preserve these invaluable works in the largest online archive of its kind. Contributions from major world libraries constitute over 175,000 original printed works. Scanned images of the actual pages, rather than transcriptions, recreate the works *as they first appeared.*

Now for the first time, these high-quality digital scans of original works are available via print-on-demand, making them readily accessible to libraries, students, independent scholars, and readers of all ages.

For our initial release we have created seven robust collections to form one the world's most comprehensive catalogs of 18th century works.

Initial Gale ECCO Print Editions collections include:

History and Geography

Rich in titles on English life and social history, this collection spans the world as it was known to eighteenth-century historians and explorers. Titles include a wealth of travel accounts and diaries, histories of nations from throughout the world, and maps and charts of a world that was still being discovered. Students of the War of American Independence will find fascinating accounts from the British side of conflict.

Social Science

Delve into what it was like to live during the eighteenth century by reading the first-hand accounts of everyday people, including city dwellers and farmers, businessmen and bankers, artisans and merchants, artists and their patrons, politicians and their constituents. Original texts make the American, French, and Industrial revolutions vividly contemporary.

Medicine, Science and Technology

Medical theory and practice of the 1700s developed rapidly, as is evidenced by the extensive collection, which includes descriptions of diseases, their conditions, and treatments. Books on science and technology, agriculture, military technology, natural philosophy, even cookbooks, are all contained here.

Literature and Language

Western literary study flows out of eighteenth-century works by Alexander Pope, Daniel Defoe, Henry Fielding, Frances Burney, Denis Diderot, Johann Gottfried Herder, Johann Wolfgang von Goethe, and others. Experience the birth of the modern novel, or compare the development of language using dictionaries and grammar discourses.

Religion and Philosophy

The Age of Enlightenment profoundly enriched religious and philosophical understanding and continues to influence present-day thinking. Works collected here include masterpieces by David Hume, Immanuel Kant, and Jean-Jacques Rousseau, as well as religious sermons and moral debates on the issues of the day, such as the slave trade. The Age of Reason saw conflict between Protestantism and Catholicism transformed into one between faith and logic -- a debate that continues in the twenty-first century.

Law and Reference

This collection reveals the history of English common law and Empire law in a vastly changing world of British expansion. Dominating the legal field is the *Commentaries of the Law of England* by Sir William Blackstone, which first appeared in 1765. Reference works such as almanacs and catalogues continue to educate us by revealing the day-to-day workings of society.

Fine Arts

The eighteenth-century fascination with Greek and Roman antiquity followed the systematic excavation of the ruins at Pompeii and Herculaneum in southern Italy; and after 1750 a neoclassical style dominated all artistic fields. The titles here trace developments in mostly English-language works on painting, sculpture, architecture, music, theater, and other disciplines. Instructional works on musical instruments, catalogs of art objects, comic operas, and more are also included.

The BiblioLife Network

This project was made possible in part by the BiblioLife Network (BLN), a project aimed at addressing some of the huge challenges facing book preservationists around the world. The BLN includes libraries, library networks, archives, subject matter experts, online communities and library service providers. We believe every book ever published should be available as a high-quality print reproduction; printed on-demand anywhere in the world. This insures the ongoing accessibility of the content and helps generate sustainable revenue for the libraries and organizations that work to preserve these important materials.

The following book is in the "public domain" and represents an authentic reproduction of the text as printed by the original publisher. While we have attempted to accurately maintain the integrity of the original work, there are sometimes problems with the original work or the micro-film from which the books were digitized. This can result in minor errors in reproduction. Possible imperfections include missing and blurred pages, poor pictures, markings and other reproduction issues beyond our control. Because this work is culturally important, we have made it available as part of our commitment to protecting, preserving, and promoting the world's literature.

GUIDE TO FOLD-OUTS MAPS and OVERSIZED IMAGES

The book you are reading was digitized from microfilm captured over the past thirty to forty years. Years after the creation of the original microfilm, the book was converted to digital files and made available in an online database.

In an online database, page images do not need to conform to the size restrictions found in a printed book. When converting these images back into a printed bound book, the page sizes are standardized in ways that maintain the detail of the original. For large images, such as fold-out maps, the original page image is split into two or more pages

Guidelines used to determine how to split the page image follows:

• Some images are split vertically; large images require vertical and horizontal splits.
• For horizontal splits, the content is split left to right.
• For vertical splits, the content is split from top to bottom.
• For both vertical and horizontal splits, the image is processed from top left to bottom right.

DRUNKEN BARNABY'S
FOUR JOURNEYS
TO THE
NORTH of ENGLAND.

In Latin and English Metre.

Wittily and merrily (tho' an Hundred Years ago) compos'd, found among some old musty Books that had lain a long Time by in a Corner, and now at last made public.

TOGETHER WITH
BESSY BELL.

---

*Hic est quem quæris, ille quem requiris,
Toto notus in Orbe—* Britannus.   Mart.
BARNABAS Ebrius.

The FOURTH EDITION,
Illustrated with several Neat Copper-Plates.

L O N D O N:
Printed by W. STUART, Nº. 67
PATER-NOSTER-ROW.

MDCCLXXIV.

THE
PREFACE
TO THE
READER.

*I*T *will not, I hope, be thought Un-*
neceſſary, if I lay before the Reader
my Reaſon for republiſhing this fa-
cetious little Book, after a deliteſcency
of near a Hundred Years. Being de-
ſir'd by a Gentlewoman *to look over*
                                    a Par-

To the Reader.

a Parcel of Old Books, among 'em I chanc'd upon DRUNKEN BARNABY, which reading gave me Satisfaction for my Trouble; whereupon I took a Resolution to publish it, that others might therewith be pleas'd as well as myself. What I can gather of the Author is chiefly from himself; for he says, Coming to a Place call'd Harrington, he was well pleas'd with the Omen, and spent some Money there for Name-sake, so that I conclude his Name was BARNABY HARRINGTON. He further says, that after a tedious Journey of about Six Miles a Day, and sometimes Three

or

To the Reader.

or Four, (very weary, and heavy laden) he at laſt arriv'd at Appleby in Weſtmoreland, where he was born, and where, if I miſtake not, there are ſome Remains of the Family ſtill living. That he was a Graduate in Queen's College, Oxon, *is plain, but I have not had an Opportunity of knowing what Degrees he took.* 'Tis the Man, no doubt, of whom the Song ſays,

Hey *Barnaby!* take't for a Warning, &c.

He ſays, he afterwards (after Four Journeys backward and forward) married in the Country, turn'd Farmer,

a   *and*

To the Reader.

and frequented the Horse-Fairs all round the Country, buying Horses when cheap, and (like a true Jockey) selling them when dear, upon which he is very pleasant. I thought fit to say thus much, and more I have not, only wish the Reader *pleas'd, as I was.*

Editor

Editor Lectori.

QUUM primum reperi libellum hunc lepidiſſimum legendo gaudebam, quod & tu facies cum legeris nullus dubito. Editum inveni abſq; æra, abſq; nominè vel Authoris, vel Bibliopolæ, vel Typographi, aut ullo alio indicio poſſeſſorem ullum indicante, ergo ſtatui mei juris eſſe, inq; lucem emiſi. De Authore quod certum eſt ſubjiciam:

Ab

Editor Lectori.

Ab amico meo doctiſſimo nunc præſule intellexi Authorem Barnabam Harrington fuiſſe ante multos annos (forte nonaginta aut centum) vel Socium, vel Artium Magiſtrum, aut ſaltem Membrum Collegii Reginenſis apud *Oxonienſes,* quod innuit etiam Authore ſæpius. Natus erat, ut ait ipſe, Aballabæ Weſtmarorum inter Septentriones ex antiqua ſtirpe, prole ibi adhuc manente. Hic eſt famoſiſſimus ille de quo decantatum illud & tritum apud vulgus cantillatur,

Hey Barnaby ! *take't for a Warning,*
Be no more drunk nor dry in a Morning.

De Libro nulla eſt neceſſitas addendi quidquam, facile perleges,
&

Editor Lectori.

& perlecto Judicabis. De Verſu, de Metro, de Erroribus neq; eſt quod addam, ipſe enim Autor ſatis ludicre in Errata libro præfixa ſeipſum vindicavit, quum ait,

> Quid ſi ſedem muto ſede ?
> Quid ſi Carmen claudo pede ?
> Quid ſi noctem ſenſi diem ?
> Quid ſi veprem eſſe viam ?
> Sat eſt, Verbum declinavi,
> " *Titubo, titubas, titubavi.*"

Vale & ride affatim, Lector.

Loyal

Loyal PHEANDER

TO HIS

Royal ALEXANDER.

THE Title, Noble Friend, of *Ale-xander*,
Were it nought elfe, implies a great *Com-
mandei* .
And fo you fhall be ftill of me and mine,
With *Barnaby* couch'd in a reeling Rhime :
Nor wonder, Friend, if his Dimenfions reel,
Whofe *Head* makes fuch Iambicks with his
Heel.

BARNABÆ
ITINERARIUM,

MIRTILI & FAUSTULI

NOMINIBUS INSIGNITUM·

Viatoris Solatio nuperrimè editum, aptiſſimis numeris redactum, veterique Tono BARNABÆ publicè decantatum.

Authore CORYMBÆO.

L O N D I N I

IMPENSIS AB ANNO 1774·

BARNABY'S JOURNAL,

UNDER THE NAMES OF

MIRTILUS and *FAUSTULUS*

SHADOW'D:

For the Traveller's Solace lately publifh'd, to moft apt Numbers reduc'd, and to the old Tune of BARNABY commonly chanted.

By CORYMBÆUS.

LONDON

PRINTED IN THE YEAR 1774.

In ERRATA.

LEctor, *ne mireris illa,*
Villam si mutavi villa,
Si regressum feci metro,
Retro ante, ante retro
Inserendo, " ut præpono
Godmanchester Harringtono.
Quid si breves *fiant* longi?
Si vocales *sint* diphthongi?
Quid si graves *sint* acuti?
Si accentus *fiant* muti?
Quid si placide, plene, plane,
Fregi frontem Prisciani?
Quid si sedem muto sede?
Quid si Carmen claudo pede?
Quid si noctem sensi diem?
Quid si veprem esse viam?
Sat est, Verbum declinavi,
" Titubo, titubas, titubavi."

A D

Upon the ERRATA's.

REader, think no Wonder by it,
  If with Town I've Town supplied;
If my Metre's backward Nature
Set before what shou'd be later.
" As for Instance is exprest there,
Harrington after *Godmanchester*
What tho' *Breve's* be made *Longo's*,
What tho' *Vowels* be *Diphthongo's*
What tho' *Graves* become *Acute* too?
What tho' *Accents* become *mute* too?
What tho' freely, fully, plainly,
I've broke *Priscian's* Forehead mainly?
What tho' Seat with Seat I've strained?
What tho' my limp Verse be maimed?
What tho' Night I've ta'en for Day too?
What tho' I've made Briers my Way too?
Know ye, I've declin'd most bravely,
"' *Titubo, titubas, titubavi.*"

TO

AD

VIATOREM.

Oppida dum peragras, pera-
grando Poemata spectes,
Spectando titubes, Barnabe, nomen habes.

AD

TO THE

TRAVELLER.

TOwns while thou walk'ſt
And ſee'ſt this Poetry,
And ſeeing, ſtumbleſt,
Thou art BARNABY.

A D

TRANSLATOREM.

PEssimus est Cerdo, qui tran-
    stulit ordine calvo,

Non res sed voces percutiendo
    leves,

Ast hic Translator corii perama-
    bilis Actor,

Quirythmo pollens fit ratione
    satur.

In-

TO THE
TRANSLATOR.

THat paltry Patcher is
a bold Tranſlator,

Whoſe *Awl* bores at the *Words*
but not the *Matter* :

But *this Tranſlator* makes
good Uſe of Leather,

By ſtitching *Rhyme* and *Reaſon*
both together.

In-

Index Operis.

MUlciber, Uva, Venus,
redolens ampulla, Si-
lenus,

Effigiem titulis explicuere suis.

Sic me Parnassi *Deserta per ar-*
dua dulcis

Raptat amor——

Bar–

The INDEX *of this Work.*

VUlcan, Grape, *Venus,*
　　Bottle, *Silen*'s Hook,

Have all explained

　　The Title of this Book.

Thus through vaſt Deſarts,

　　Promontories wild,

Parnaſſus-Love draws

　　Bacchus' only Child.

B　　　　　　*Barna-*

Barnabæ Harringtoni

Et nunc & dudum decantati

ITINERARIUM

Boream quater retroverſus.

Pars Prima.

Mirtillus & *Fauſtulus* Interlocutores.

Mirtil.

O Fauſtule! *tende palmam,*
   Accipe calicem vitibus almam;
   Tunc vinctus es dolore?
Uvæ tinctus ſis colore.
Sperne opes, ſperne dapes,
Merge curas, rectè ſapis.

O Fau-

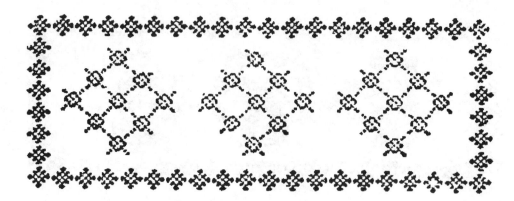

The Famous
Barnaby Harrington's
TRAVELS to the North,
Four times backward and forward.

Part the First.

Mirtillus and *Faustulus*, a Dialogue.

Mirtil.

O Little *Faustus!* stretch thy Hand out,
Take thy Liquor, do not stand out;
Art thou 'prest with griping Dolour?
Let rich Wine advance thy Colour.
Bread's a Binder, Wealth's a Miser,
Drink down Care, and thou'lt be wiser.

Little

O Faſtule, *dic amico*
Quo in loco, quo in vico,
Sive campo, sive tecto,
Sine linteo, sine lecto,
Propinaſti, queis tabernis,
An in Terris, an Avernis?

Fauſtul.

O Mirtille ! *baculum fixi*
Mille locis ubi vixi,
In piſtrinis, in popinis,
In Coquinis, in Culinis,
Huc, & illuc, iſtic, ibi,
Hauſi potus, plus quam cibi.

In progreſſu Boreali,
Ut proceſſi ab Auſtrali,
Veni Banbury, O profanum !
Ubi vidi Puritanum,

Felem

Little *Fauſtus*, tell thy true Heart,
In what Region, Coaſt, or new Part;
Field or Fold thou haſt been bouſing,
Without Linen, Bedding, Houſing;
In what Tavern, pray thee ſhow us,
Here on Earth, or elſe below us?

Fauſtus.

O *Mirtillus!* I will ſhew thee
Thouſand Places ſince I ſaw thee,
In the Bakehouſe I had ſwitching,
In the Tap-houſe, Cook-ſhop, Kitchen;
This Way, that Way, each Way ſhrank I,
Little eat I, deeply drank I.

In my Progreſs travelling Northward,
Taking farewell of the Southward,
To *Banbury* came I, O prophane-One!
Where I ſaw a Puritane-One

Felem facientem furem,
Quod Sabbatho stravit Murem.

Veni Oxon, *cui comes*
Est Minerva, *fons* Platonis ;
Unde scatent peramœne
Aganippe, Hippocrene ;
Totum fit Atheniense,
Imo Cornu Riginense.

Inde Godstow, *cum Amicis,*
Vidi Tumbam Meretricis ;
Rosamundam *tegit humus,*
Pulvis & umbra corpore sumus ,
Sic qui teget, quæ tegetur,
Ordine certo sepelietur.

Inde Woodstock, *quo spectandum*
Labyrinthum memorandum
Ferunt , sed spectare nollem,
Reperi vivam Hospitem mollem ;

G 3 a-

Hanging of his Cat on Monday,
For killing of a Mouſe on Sunday.

To *Oxford* came I, whoſe Companion
Is *Minerva*, Well *Platonian :*
From whoſe Seat do ſtream moſt ſeemly,
Aganippe, Hippocrene ;
Each thing there's the *Muſe's Minion,*
The Horn at Queens ſpeaks pure *Athenian.*

Thence to *Godſtow,* with my Lovers,
Where a Tomb a Strumpert covers ,
Roſamund lies there interr'd,
Fleſh to Duſt and Shades compar'd ;
Lie he above, or lie ſhe under,
To be bury'd is no wonder.

Thence to *Woodſtock* I reſorted,
Where a Labyrinth's reported ;
No more of that, it is above me,
I found a tender Houſewife that did love me ;

And

Barnabæ Itinerarium.

Gratior sociis est jocundis,
Mille mortuis Rosamundis.

Veni Barkley, ubi natus
Stirpe vili Magistratus,
Quem conspexi residentem,
Stramine tectum contegentem,
Et me vocans, "Male agis,
"Bibe minus, ede magis.

Veni Daintree cum puella,
Procerum celebre duello.
Ibi bibi in Caupona,
Nota muliere bona,
Cum qua vixi semper idem,
Donec creta fregit fidem.

Veni Leicester ad Campanam,
Ubi mentem læfi sanam,
Prima nocte mille modis
Flagellarunt me Custodes,

Pelle

And her Guefts more fweetly eyeing,
Than thoufand *Rofamonds* a dy ng.

From thence to *Barkley*, as did befeem one,
The May'r I faw, a wond'rous mean one,
Sitting, Thatching, and beftowing
On a Wind blown Houfe a Strawing,
On me call'd he, and did charm me,
" Drink lefs, eat more, I do warn thee."

Thence to *Daintree* with my *Jewel*,
Famous for a *Noble Duel*,
Where I drank, and took my Common
In a Tap-houfe with my Woman:
While I had it, there I paid it,
Till long *chalking* broke my Credit.

Thence I came to th' *Bell* at *Leicefter*,
Where ftrong Ale my Brains did pefter;
Firft Night befure I was admitted
By the Watchmen I was whipped,

Black

Pelle sparsi sunt livores
Meos castigare mores.

   Veni Gotham, *ubi multos*
Si non omnes vidi stultos,
Nam scrutando reperi unam
Salientem contra Lunam,
Alteram nitidum puellam
Offerentem Porco sellam.

   Veni * Nottingham, *tyrones*
Sherwoodenses *sunt Latrones,*

                        Instar

---

* Mortimeriados morti dos, Gloria Pulvis,
   Atria sunt frondes, Nobilis Aula seges.
Nunc gradus Anfractus, Cisterna fluenta spadonis,
   Amplexus Vermes, oscula mista rogis.

Clamat Tempus edo, vocemque repercutit Echo,
   Sed Nunquam redeo, voce Resurgit ego.

O vos Heroes! attendite fata Sepulchris,
   Heroum, patriis qui Rediere thoris!
Non estis luti Melioris in orbe Superbis,
   Hi Didicere mori, discite morte sequi.

Black and Blue like any Tetter,
Beat I was to make me Better.

Thence to *Gotham*, where, sure am I,
Though not all Fools, I saw many ;
Here a She-Bull found I prancing,
And in Moon-shine nimbly dancing :
There another wanton mad one,
Who her Hog was set astride on.

Thence to * *Nottingham*, where Rovers,
Highway Riders, *Sherwood* Drovers,

Like

---

* Brave *Mortimer's* now dead, his Glory Dust,
His Courts are clad with Grass, his Hall with Rust,
His Stairs steep Steps, his Horse-troughs Cisterns are,
Worms his Embraces, Kisses Ashes share.

Time cries, *I eat*, and Eccho answers it :
But gone, e'er to return, is held unfit.

O Heroes ! of these Heroes take a view ;
They're to their Fathers gone, and so must you '
Of better Clay you are not than these Men,
And they are dead, and you must follow them.

Inftar Robin Hood *& Servi*
Scarlet *&* Joannis Parvi ;
Paffim, fparfim peculantur,
Cellis, Sylvis deprædantur.

Veni Mansfield, *ubi noram*
Mulierculam decoram,
Cum qua nudum feci pactum.
Dedi ictum, egi actum,
Sed pregnantem timens illam,
Sprevi villam & ancillam.

Veni * Overbowles, *ubi* † Dani
Habitarunt tempore Jani,
Pater oppidanus callis
Circumcirca claufus vallis,

Caftris,

---

* Temporibus Jani Sedes fuit ultima † Dani,
Confpicuis vallis obfita, fixa palis.

Like old *Robin Hood*, and *Scarlet*,
Or like Little *John* his Varlet;
Here and there they shew them Doughty,
In Cells and Woods to get their Booty.

Thence to *Mansfield*, Where I knew one,
That was a comely and a true one,
With her a naked Compact made I,
Her long lov'd I, with her laid I;
Town and her I left both, doubtful
Left my Love had made her fruitful.

Thence to * *Overbowles*, where † *Danus*
Dwelt with's *Danes* in time of *Janus*;
Way to th' Town is well difpos'd,
All about with Trenches clos'd;

Pallifa-

---

* In *Janus* time was † *Danus* feated here,
  As by their Pales and Trenches may appear.

Castris, claustris, & speluncis
Tectus cœcis, tectus juncis.
Sacra die eò veni,
Ædes Sanctæ erant plenæ,
Quorum percitus exemplo,
Quia Hospes erat Templo,
Intrans vidi Sacerdotem,
Igne fatuo *poculis notum.*

Glires erant incolæ villæ,
Iste clamat, dormiunt illi ;
Ipse tamen vixit ita,
Si non corde, veste trita ;
Fortem præ se ferens gestum,
Fregit pedibus * Suggestum.
Qua Occasione nacta
Tota grex † expurgefacta,

Sacer–

---

* Fragmina suggesti sacrarunt fercula festi.

Lucret

† O cives, cives, Sacris attendite rivis,
Præceptor legerit, vos vero negligitis.

Pallifadoes hid with Bufhes,
Rampires overgrown with Rufhes.
On a Feaft-day I came thither,
When Good People flock'd together,
Where (induc'd by Hoft's example)
I repair'd unto the Temple,
Where I heard the Preacher gravely,
With his red Nofe tipt moft bravely.

Dormice-like the People feem'd,
Though he cry'd, they fleeping dream'd;
For his Life, tho' there was harm in't,
Heart was lefs rent than his Garment:
With his Feet he did fo thunder,
That the * Pulpit fell afunder.
Which Occafion having gotten
All † awake, the Pulpit broken,

While

---

* The fragments of which Pulpit they were pleas'd
  To facrifice to th' Afhes of their Feaft.   *Lucret.*
† Pray you, good Townfmen, fecred Springs affect,
  Let not your Preacher *read*, and you *neglect*.

Sacerdote derelicto,
Tabulis fractis graviter icto,
Pransum redeunt, unus horum,
Plebem sequor non Pastorem.

Veni Clowne, *ubi vellem*
Pro liquore dare pellem,
Ibi cerebro inani
Vidi Conjugem Vulcani,
Quæ me Hospitem tractat bene
Donec restat nil crumenæ.

Veni Rothram *usque* Taurum,
Et reliqui ibi Aurum,
Diu steti, sed in pontem
Titubando fregi frontem,
Quo pudore pulsus, docte
Clam putabam ire nocte.

Veni Doncaster, *ubi sitam*
Vidi levem & Levitam,

Quæ

While the Preacher lay fore wounded,
With more Boards than Beards furrounded;
All to Dinner, who might fafter,
So among them I left Paftor.

Thence to *Clowne* I came the quicker,
Where I'd given my Skin for Liquor;
None was there to entertain us,
But a Nogging of *Vulcanus*,
Who afford't me Welcome plenty,
Till my Seam-rent Purfe was empty.

Thence to th' *Bull* at *Rothram* came I,
Where my Gold, if I had any,
Left I, long I ftoutly roared,
Till on Bridge I broke my Forehead,
Whence afham'd, while Forehead fmarted,
I by Night-time thence departed.

Thence to *Donc'fter*, who'll believe it?
Both a *Light-one* and a *Levite*,

There

Quæ vieta & vetusta,
Parum pulchra aut venusta,
Cupit tamen penetrari,
Pingi, pungi, osculari.

Veni * Aberford, *ubi notum*
Quod aciculis emunt potum,
Pauperes sunt & indigentes,
Multum tamen sitientes;
Parum habent, nec habentur
Ulla, quæ non tenet venter.

Veni

---

* Eo tempore, quo in hoc pauperiore Vico hospitium suscepimus quidam Acicularius, è grege præ cæteris, fama egregius, aciculari pulvere suffocatus interiit; in cujus memoriam hoc inscriptum comperimus Epitaphium:

———— O Mors crudelis!
Quæ tuis telis
   Artificem stravisti
Qui meliorem
Erasit pulverem
   Quam tu de eo fecisti.

There I view'd; too, too aged,
Yet to Love fo far engaged,
That on Earth fhe only wifhed
To be painted, pricked, kiffed.

Thence to * *Aberford,* whofe Beginning
Came from buying Drink with Pinning :
Poor they are, and very needy,
Yet of Liquor very greedy :
Had they never fo much Plenty,
Belly'd make their Purfes empty.

C 2

Thence

----

* At fuch Time as we fojourn'd in this poor
Village, it chanc'd that a certain Pinner, and
of the choiceft of all his Flock, being choak'd
with Pin-duft, dy'd ; to whofe Memory we find
this Epitaph recorded .

———— O cruel Death !
To rob this Man of Breath,
Who, while he liv'd, in fcraping of a Pin,
Made better Duft than thou haft made of him.

Veni * Wetherb, *ubi visam*
Clari Ducis meretricem,
Amplexurus, porta strepit,
Et strependo Dux me cepit ,
Ut me cepit, aurem vellit,
Et præcepitem foris pellit.

    Hinc diverso cursu, sero
Quod audissem de Pindero
Wakefeeldensi, *gloria Mund',*
Ubi socii sunt jucundi,
Mecum statui peragrare
Georgii *fustem visitare.*

Veni Wakefeeld *peramænum,*
Ubi quærens Georgium Grenum,
Non inveni, sed in lignum
Fixum reperi Georgii *signum,*

                                           Ubi

---

* In Corneolo Angiportu,
   Subamœniore Hortu
   Speciosa manet scorta,
   Meretricia Procans sporta.

'Thence to * *Wetherb*, where an apt one
'To be *Punk* unto a Captain
I embrac'd, as I had got it,
But Door creak'd, and Captain fmoak'd it:
Took me by th' Ears, and fo drew me,
Till head-long down Stairs he threw me.

Turning thence, none cou'd me hinder
To falute the *Wakefield Pindar*;
Who indeed is the World's Glory,
With his *Comrades* never forry,
This was the Caufe, left you fhould mifs it,
George's Club I meant to vifit

Strait at *Wakefield* I was feen a,
Where I fought for *George à Green* a,
But cou'd find not fuch a Creature,
Yet on a Sign I faw his Feature,

C 3

Where

---

* Near *Horn-Alley*, in a Garden,
A Wench more wanton than *Kate Arden*,
Sojourns, one that fcorns a Waft-coat,
Wooing Clients with her Bafket

Ubi allam bibi feram,
Donec Georgio fortior eram.

   Veni Bradford, *ceſſi foris*
In Familiam Amoris,
Amant iſtæ & amantur,
Creſcunt & multiplicantur,
Spiritus inſtructi armis,
Nocte colunt opera carnis.

   Veni Kighley, *ubi montes*
Mintantes, vivi fontes,
Ardui colles, aridæ valles,
Læti tamen ſunt Sodales,
Feſtivantes & jucundi,
Ac ſi Domini eſſent Mundi.

   Veni Gigglefwick, *parum frugis*
Profert tellus clauſa jugis ,

Where Strength of Ale had so much stir'd me,
That I grew stouter far than *Jordie.*

Thence to *Bradford,* where I enter'd,
In Family where Love oft center'd .
They love, are lov'd, and make no Shew,
Yet still grow, and do encrease too :
Furnish'd with their sprightly Weapons;
She-flesh feels Priests are no Capons.

Thence to *Kighley,* where are Mountains,
Steepy-threatning, lively Fountains;
Rising Hills, and barren Vallies,
Yet *Bon-Socio*'s and good Fellows ,
Jovial, jocund, jolly Bowlers,
As they were the World's Controulers.

Thence to *Gigglesvick* most steril,
Hemm'd with Rocks and Shelves of Peril .

Near

Ibi * *vena prope viæ*
Fluit, refluit, nocte, diu,
Neque nôrunt unde vena,
An à sale vel arena.

Veni Clapham, *unus horum*
Qri accivit voce forum,
Prima hora ut me visit,
Mihi Halecem promisit,
Halecem mihi, calicem ei,
Pignus in amoris mei

Veni † Ingleton, *ubi degi*
Donec Fabri caput fregi,
Quo peracto, in me ruunt
Mulieres, saxa pluunt,

Q Ieis

---

* E gremio collis saliens scatet unda perennis,
　Quæ fluit & refluit, nil tamen æstus habet.

† Pirgus inest fano, fanum sub acumine Collis,
　Collis ab elatis actus & actus auctus Aquis

Near to th' Way as a Traveller goes,
A fresh * Spring both ebbs and flows:
Neither know the Learn'd that travel,
What procures it, *Salt* or *Gravel.*

Thence to *Clapham,* drawing nigher,
He that was the common Cryer
☞ To a Breakfast of one Herring
Did invite me first appearing
Herring he, I Drink bestow'd,
Pledges of the Love we ow'd.

Thence to † *Ingleton,* where I liv'd
Till I brake a Blacksmith's Head,
Which done, Women rush'd in on me,
Stones like Hail shower'd down upon me:

Whence

---

* Near th' bottom of this Hill, close by the Way,
  A fresh Spring ebbs and flows all Hours o'th' Day

† The Poor-man's Box is in the Temple set,
  Church under Hill, the Hill by Waters bet

Queis perculſus, timens lædi,
His poſteriora dedi.

    Veni Lonesdale, *ubi cernam*
Aulam factam in Tabernam,
Nitidæ portæ, nivei muri,
Cyathi pleni, paucæ curæ;
Edunt, bibunt, ludunt, rident,
Cura dignum nihil vident.

    Veni Cowbrow, *vaccæ collem,*
Ubi hoſpitem tetigi mollem,
Pingui ventre, læto vultu,
Tremulo curſu, trepido cultu,
Uti bibula titubat Vates,
Donec cecidit ſupra nates.

    Veni Natland, *eo ventus,*
Eboraci *qui Contemptus*
Colligit, hoſpitium dedit,
Mecum bibit, mecum edit,

                                    Semi

Whence aſtoniſh'd fearing harming,
Leave I took, but gave no Warning.

Thence to *Loneſdale*, where I view'd
An Hall, which like a Tavern ſhew'd;
Neat Gates, white Walls, nought was ſparing,
Pots brimfull, no thought of careing
They eat, drink, laugh, are ſtill Mirth-making,
Nought they ſee that's worth Care taking.

Thence to *Cowbrow*, Truth I'll tell ye,
Mine Hoſteſs had a ſupple Belly,
Body plump, and Count'nance chearful,
Reeling Peace (a Welcome fearful)
Like a drunken Hag ſhe ſtumbled,
Till ſhe on her Buttocks tumbled.

Thence to *Natland*, b'ing come thither,
He who *York*'s Contempts did gather,
Gave me Harbour light as Feather,
We both drank and eat together,

Till

Semipotus, ficut ufi,
Circa May-pole *plebe lufi.*

   Veni Kirkland, *veni* Kendall,
Omnia haufi, vulgo Spend-all,
Nocte, die, peramicè
Bibi potum miftum pice.
  " *Tege caput, tende manum,*
  " *Manu caput fit infanum.*"

   His relictis, Staveley *vidi,*
Ubi tota Nocte bibi,
Semper lepidus, femper lætus,
Inter hilares vixi Cœtus,
Queis jurando fum manfurus,
Donec Barnabæ *rediturus.*

Till half tipſy, as it chanced,
We about the *May-pole* danced.

Thence to *Kirkland,* thence to *Kendall,*
I did that which Men call *Spend-all:*
Night and Day with Sociates many,
I drank Ale both thick and clammy.
" Shroud thy Head Boy, ſtretch thy Hand too,
" Hand has done what Head can't ſtand to."

Leaving theſe, to *Staveley* came I,
Where now all Night drinking am I,
Always frolick, free from Yellows,
With a Conſort of good Fellows ;
Where I'll ſtay, and end my Journey,
Till Brave *Barnaby* return a.

THE END OF THE FIRST PART.

In BACCHI *Thyrsum* & BAR-
NABÆ *Nasum*;

E P I G R A M M A:

A L I A S,

Nasutum Dilemma.

HÆdera læta bono non est suspensa salei no,
Thyrsus enim Bacchi, Barnabæ Nasus erit.
Non opus est Thyrso, non frondi virent cupressi,
Si non Thyrsus erit, Barnabæ Nasus olet.

Corollarium.

Non Thyrsus, Thyasus; Cyathus tibi Thyrsus &
Ursus,
Thyrsus quo redoles Ursus ut intus oles.

Upon

Upon BACCHUS's *Bush and* BAR-
NABY's *Nose*;

An E P I G R A M :

O R,   T H E

Long-snouted Dilemma.

Good Wine no Bush doth need, as I suppose,
Let *Bacchus* Bush be *Barnaby*'s rich Nose.
No Bush, no Garland needs of Cypress green,
Barnaby's Nose may for a Bush be seen.

Corollary.

No Bush, no Garland; Pot's thy *Bush* and *Bear* :
Of *Bear* and *Bush* thou smellest all the Year.

Bar--

Barnabæ Itinerarium.

PARS II.

Mirtil.

FAuste (Faſtule) rediſti,
    Narra (precor) quo veniſti,
Villos, vicos viſitaſti,
Cœtus, Situs peragraſti,
Certe ſcis ab Aquilone,
Multum mali, parvum boni.

Fauſtul.

Barnaby's Journal.

PART II.

Mirtil.

YOUNG *Faufte*, happily returned;
　Tell me, prithee, where'ft fojourned;
What Towns, Villages thou'ft viewed,
What Seats, Sights, or States were fhewed:
Sure thou know'ft the *North*'s uncivil,
Small Good comes thence, but much Evil.

Fauſtul.

Ille ego ſum qui quondam,
Crines, mores, veſtes nondum
Sunt mutatæ, nam receſſi,
Calceamentis queis diſceſſi,
Neque pectine uſus fui,
Sic me meis juvat frui.
Sed arrectis auribus audi,
Quid dilexi, quicquid odi,
* *Pontes, Fontes, Montes, Valles,*
Caulas, Cellas, Colles, Calles,
Vias, Villas, Vicos, Vices,
Caſtas, cautas, meretrices.
Dicam (quod mirandum) verum,
Non pauperior ſum quam eram,
Uno nec quadrante ditior,
Lautior, lætior, nec fælicior,
Mollior, melior, potior, pejor,
Minus ſanus, magis æger.

Ego

---

* Anglia, mons, fons, pons, Ecclefia, fœmina, lana.

Faustul.

What I was once, fame I am now,
Hair, Conditions, Garments too;
Yea, there's no Man juftly doubteth,
Thefe the fame Shoes I went out with :
And for Comb I ne'er us'd any,
Left I loft fome of my Money.
But attend me, and partake it,
What I loved, what I hated,
* Bridges, Fountains, Mountains, Vallies,
Huts, Cells, Hillocks, Highways, Shallows,
Paths, Towns, Villages, and Trenches,
Chafte, choice, chary, merry Wenches.
Truth I'll tell thee, nothing furer,
Richer am not, nor yet poorer;
Gladder, madder, nor more pleafing,
Blither, brifker, more in Seafon;
Better, worfer, thinner, thicker,
Neither healthier nor ficker.

D 2

For

---

* *England*, amongft all Nations, is moft full
Of Hills, Wells, Bridges, Churches, Women, Wool.

Ego enim Mundum totum
Tanti esse quanti potum
Semper duxi   mori mallem
Nobilem quam vitare allam.
" *Sobrius similis apparet Agno,*
" *Ebrius* Alexandro Magno."
Leviore nam Mæandro
Capite capto, sum Lysandro
Multo fortior, & illæsum
Puto me capturum Rhesum :
Sed ne tibi gravior essem,
Nunc descendam ad Progressum.

  Primò occurrit peregranti
* *Oppidum* Joannis Ganti,
Sedes nota & vetusta,
Mendicantibus onusta,

Jani-

---

* Scinditur à clivo Turris, bitumine murus ;
  Mœnia sic propriis funt reddatura rogis.

For the World, I fo far prize it,
But for Liquor I'd defpife it .
Thoufand Deaths I'd rather die too,
Than old Ale mine Enemy too :
" Sober, Lamb-like do I wander,
" Drunk, I'm ftout as *Alexander.*"
When my Head feels its Mæander,
I am ftronger than *Lyfander* ·
Th' Ifle of *Ree*, I little fear it,
Without Wound to win and wear it :
But left tedious I exprefs me,
To my *Progrefs* I'll addrefs me.

Firft Place where I firft was known-a,
Was Brave *John à Gant*'s old * Town-a :
A Seat antiently renowned,
But with ftore of Beggars crowned ,

D 3

For

---

* An antient Arch doth threaten a decline,
   And fo muft ftrongeft Piles give way to *Time.*

Janitorem *habens qualem*
Mundus vix ostendet talem

   Veni Afhton, *ubi vidi*,
Militem, & Heroinam,
Clarum, charum, & formosam,
Damam, domum speciosam
Vidi, merfi mero Musam,
Donec pes amifit ufum.

   Veni Garftang, *ubi male*
Intrans forum Beftiale,
Forte vacillando vico
Huc & illuc cum amico,
In Juvencæ dorfum rui
Cujus cornu læfus fui.

   Veni Prefton, *ductus eram*
Ad bacchantem Banifterum,
Ac fi una ftirpe nati,
Fratres fuimus jurati;

For a *Gaoler* ripe and mellow,
The World has not fuch a Fellow.

Thence to *Afhton*, good as may be
Was the Wine, brave Knight, bright Lady;
All I faw was comely, fpecious,
Seemly gracious, neatly precious;
My Mufe with *Bacchus* fo long traded,
When I walk'd, my Legs deny'd it.

Thence to *Garflang*, pray you hark it,
Ent'ring there a great Beaft-market;
As I jogged on the Street,
'Twas my Fortune for to meet
A young Heifer, who before her
Took me up, and threw me o'er her.

Thence to *Prefton*, I was led-a,
To Brave *Banifter*'s to Bed-a;
As two born and bred together,
We were prefently fworn Brether:

Seven

Septem dies ibi mansi,
Multum bibi, nunquam pransi.

Veni Euston, ubi hospes
Succi plena, corpore sospes,
Crine sparso, vultu blando,
At halitu (proh) nefando,
Qua relicta cum ancillis,
Me ad lectum duxit Phillis.

Veni Wigan prope cœnam,
Ad hospitulam obscœnam ;
Votis meis fit secunda,
Ebria fuit & jocunda ;
Sparsit anus intellectum,
Me relicto, minxit lectum.

Veni Newton in Salictis,
Ubi ludens chartis pictis
Cum puella speciosa,
Cujus nomen erat * Rosa,

Centi-

---

* Quam *Rosa* spiravit! sed odoribus *Aquilo* flavit,
  Et rugas retulit quas meminisse dolet.

Seven Days were there affigned,
Oft I Supt, but never Dined

Thence to *Eufton*, where mine Hoftefs
Feels as foft as any Toaft is :
Juicy, lufty, Count'nance toothfome ;
Braided Hair, but Breath moft loathfome ;
Her I left with Locks of Amber ;
Plyllis light me to my Chamber.

Thence to *Wigan* about Supper,
To an Hoftefs, none more flutter :
Buxom was fhe, yet to fee to,
She'd be drunk for Company too ;
Wit this Beldame foon did fcatter,
And in Bed diftill'd her Water.

Thence to *Newton* in the *Willows*,
Where being boulfter'd up with Pillows,
I at Cards play'd with a Girl,
⁂ *Rofe* by Name, a dainty Pearl :

At

⁂ Frefh was my *Rofe*, till by a North Wind tofs'd,
She Sap, Scent, Verdure, and her Vigour loft.

Centi-pede provocavi
Ad amandum quam amavi.

   Veni Warrington, *profluentes*
Rivos ripas transeuntes
Spectans, multo satius ratus
Mergi Terris quam in Aquis,
Vixi laute, bibi læte,
Donec aquas signant metæ.

   Veni Budworth *usque* Gallum,
Ubi bibi fortem allam,
Sed *ebrietate captus,*
Ire lectum sum coactus ;
Mihi minus affuit status,
A duobus sum portatus.

   Sed amore captus grandi.
Visitandi Thomam Gandi,
Holmi *petii* Sacellum,
Ubi conjugem & puellam

                                          Vidi

At Centy-foot I often moved
Her to love me, whom I loved.

Thence to *Warrington*, Banks o'erflowed,
Travellers to th' Town were rowed;
Where suppofing it much better
To be drown'd on Land than Water,
Sweetly, neatly I fojourned
Till that Deluge thence returned.

Thence to th' *Cock* at *Budworth*, where I
Drank ftrong Ale as brown as Berry;
Till at laft with deep Healths felled,
To my Bed I was compelled :
I for State was bravely forted,
By two Porters well fupported.

Where no fooner underftand I
Of mine honeft Hoft *Tom Gandi*,
To *Holm-Chapel* forthwith fet I,
Maid and Hoftefs both were pretty,

Vidi pulchras, licet sero
Has neglexi, mersus mero.

    Hinc ad Tauk-a-Hill *perventum,*
Collem valde lutulentum,
Faber mihi bene notus
Mecum bibit donec potus,
Quo relicto, Cythera *sponte*
Cornua fixit Lemnia *fronte.*

    Novo-Castro Subter-linum.
Mulsum propinavi Vinum;
Nullus ibi fit scelestus,
Vox clamantis in suggestis;
Portas castitatis frangunt,
Quas extincta luce tangunt

    Veni Stone *ad* Campanam,
Vidi * Deliam *non* Dianam .
Hic suspectam habens vitam
Pastor gregis, Jesuitam

                              Me

---

* O mellea mea Delia !

But to drink took I affection,
I forgot foon their Complexion.

Thence to *Tauk-a-Hill* refort I,
An Hill fteepy, flippery, dirty ·
Smith with me being well acquainted,
Drank with me till's Brains were tainted.
Having left me, *Venus* fwore it,
She'd Shooe-horn her *Vulcan*'s Forehead.

At *Newcaftle Under-line* a,
There I trounc'd it in burnt Wine a :
None o'th' *Wicked* there remained,
Weekly Lectures were proclaimed :
Chaftity they roughly handle,
While blind Zeal fnuffs out the Candle.

Thence to th' *Bell* at *Stone* ftrait drew I,
* *Delia*, no *Diana* faw I :
By the Parfon I was cited,
Who held me for Jefuited ;

In

---

* O my Honeyfuckle *Delia* !

Me cenfebat, fed incertas
Nil invenit præter chartas.

    Haywood *properans malignam,*
Nocte præparat aprugnam
Mihi Hofpes; fed quid reftat?
Calices haurire præftat:
Nullum Baccho gratius libum,
Quam mutare potu cibum.

    Veni Ridgelay, *ubi Faber,*
Cui liquor Summus labor,
Mecum bibit; Nocte data
Mihi matula perforata,
Vafis crimine detecto,
Fit Oceanus in lecto.

    Veri Bruarton, Claudi *domum,*
Ubi querulum audiens fonum,
Conjugem virum verberantem,
Et vicinum equitantem;

'n his fearch, the Door faft locked,
Nought but Cards were in my Pocket.

Thence to *Haywood* taking flight-a,
Mine Hoftefs give me Brawn at Night-a :
But, what's that unto the Matter ?
Whiſkins forted with my Nature .
To brave *Bacchus* no Gift quicker
Than Meat changed to ftrong Liquor.

Thence to *Ridgelay*, where a Blackſmith
(Liquor being all he'd take with)
Bouzed with me ; Midnight waking,
And a Looking-glaſs there taking,
Chamber-pot was hol'd quite thorow,
Which made me lie wet till Morrow.

Thence to *Bruarton*, old *Claudus*
Did approve us and applaud us ;
Where I heard a woful bleating,
A curft Wife her Huſband beating :

Neigh-

Quo peracto, frontem lini
Spuma bynes instar vini.

Inde * Litchfield *properabam,*
Ubi quendam invitabam
Perobscænum opibus plenum,
Ad sumendum mecum cœnam ;
Hausto vino, acta cœna,
Solvit divitis crumena.

Veni Coleshill, *ad macellum,*
Ubi in cervisiam cellam
Forte ruens, cella sordet,
Uxor mulcet, ursa mordet ;
Sed ut Lanius fecit focum
Lectum, dereliqui locum.

Veni Meredin, *Meri-die,*
Ubi longæ fessus viæ,

Hospitem

---

* Cautibus, arboribus, cinaris, frondentibus herbis,
Crevit in Ecclesiam vallis opima tuam.

Neighbour rode for his Default-a,
While I dy'd my Front with Malt-a.

Thence to * *Litchfield* went I right on,
Where I chanced to invite one,
A Curmudgeon rich, but nafty,
To a Supper on a Pafty:
Having fipp'd, and fupp'd, and ended,
What I fpent the Mifer lended.

Thence to *Colefhill*, to a Shamble,
Like an old Fox, did I ramble
Down nafty Cellar, Wife inviting,
All while curfed Bear was biting ·
But the Butcher having made
The Fire his Bed, no more I ftaid.

Thence to *Meredin* did fteer I,
Where grown Foot-fore, and fore weary,

E   I re-

---

* Enclos'd with Cliffs, Trees, Grafs, and Artichokes,
The fruitful Vale up to the Temple looks.

E

Hospitem in genu cepi,
Et ulterius furtim repi ;
Cum qua propinando mansi,
Donec sponsam sponsum sensi.

Veni Coventry, *ubi dicunt*
Quod Cæruleum-filum *texunt,*
Ego autem hoc ignoro,
Nullum enim emi foro,
Nec discrevi juxta morem,
Lignum, lucem, nec colorem.

Veni Dunchurch *per latrones*
Ad lurcones & lenones,
Nullum tamen timui horum,
Nec latronem, nec liquorem ;
Etsi Dives metu satur,
Cantet vacuus Viator.

Mane Daintry *ut venissem,*
Corculum quod reliquissem,

Avide

I repos'd, where I chuck'd *Joan*-a
Felt her Pulfe, would further gone-a :
There we drank, and no Gueft crofs'd us,
Till I took Hoft for th' Hoftefs.

Thence to *Coventry*, where 'tis faid-a
Coventry-Blue is only made-a ;
This I know not, for fure am I,
In no Market bought I any :
Bacchus made me fuch a Scholar,
Black or Blue, I knew no Colour.

Thence to *Dunchurch*, where Report is
Of Pimps and Punks a great refort is ,
But to me none fuch appeared,
Thief nor Bung-hole I ne'er feared :
Tho' Curmudgeons have Fears plenty,
Safe he fings whofe Purfe is empty.

At *Daintry* early might you find me,
But not the Wench I left behind me :

E 2

Near

Avide quærens per musæam,
Desponsatam esse eam
Intellexi, qua audita,
" Vale (dixi) Proselyta."

Veni Wedon, ubi varii
Omnis gentis Tabellarii
Convenissent, donec mundus
Currit cerebro rotundus :
" Solvite Sodales læti,
" Plus * reliqui quam accepi."

Veni Tosseter die Martis,
Ubi Baccalaureum artis
Bacchanalia celebrantem
Ut inveni tam constantem,
Feci me consortem festi
Tota nocte perhonesti.

Veni

---

* Nauseanti Stomacho effluunt omnia.

Near the School-houſe where I bouſed,
Her I ſought, but ſhe was 'ſpouſed ;
Which I having heard that Night-a,
" Farewell (quoth I) *Proſelyta.*"

Thence to *Wedon,* where I tarry'd
In a Waggon to be carried ;
Carriers there are to be found-a,
Who will drink till th' World turns round-a
" Pay, good Fellows, I'll pay nought here,
" I have left * more than I brought here,"

Thence to *Toſſeter* on *Tueſday,*
Where an artful Batchelor choos'd I
To conſort with , we ne'er budged,
But to *Bacchus* Revels trudged :
All the Night-long ſate we at it,
Till we both grew heavy-pated.

E 3   Thence

---

* My queaſy Stomach making bold
To give them that it could not hold.

Veni Stratford, *ubi* Grenum
Procis procam, Veneris venam,
Nulla tamen forma jugis,
* *Verdor oris perit rugis;*
Flos ut viret femel arct,
Forma fpreta procis caret.

Tenens curfum & decorum,
Brickhill, *ubi* Juniorem
Veni, vidi, propter mentem
Unum octo Sapientum;
Sonat vox ut Philomela,
Ardet nafus ut candela.

Hocklahole *ut acceffiffem,*
Cellam Scyllam incidiffem,
Antro fimilem Inferni,
Aut latibulo Lavernæ;

Ibi

---

* Vere fruor titulo, non fanguine, fronte, capillo !
Nomine fi vireo, Vere tamen pero.

Thence to *Stratford*, where *Frank* * *Green*-a,
Dantieſt Doe that e'er was ſeen-a,
Venus Varniſh, me ſaluted,
But no Beauty long can ſuit it ;
Beauty feedeth, Beauty fadeth,
Beauty loſt, her Wooer 'vadeth.

Holding on my Journey longer,
Strait at *Brickhill*, with *Tom Younger*
I arriv'd, one, by this Cheeſe-a,
Stil'd the eighth Wiſe-man of *Greece*-a,
Voice more ſweet than *Progne*'s Siſter,
Like a Torch his Noſe doth gliſter.

To *Hocklayhole* as I approached,
Scylla's Barmy Cell I broached,
Dark as th' Cave of *Pluto*'s Station,
Or *Laverna*'s Habitation :

E 4

Quaffing

---

* *Green* is my Name, from him whom I obey,
But tho' my Name be green, my Head is grey.

Ibi diu propinando,
Sævior eram quam Orlando.

Veni Dunstable, *ubi mures*
Intus reptant, extus fures,
Sed vacandum omni metu
Furum temulento cœtu,
Pars ingenii mansit nulla
Quam non tenuit ampulla.

Veni Redbour, *ubi Mimi*
Neq, medii, neq; primi:
Prologus hedera redimitus
Simiano gestu situs,
* *Convivalem cecinit odem,*
Heus tu corrige diploidem.

Illinc

Actor.
* Dapes Convivio, fapore vario.

Auctor.
Diplois fpatio lataque medio,
Corrige diploidem ægregiæ Nebulo.

Quaffing there while I could ftand-o,
Madder grew I than *Orlando.*

Thence to *Dunftable,* all about me,
Mice within, and Thieves without me:
But no Fear affrights deep Drinkers,
There I tofs'd it with my Skinkers:
Not a Drop of Wit remained
Which the Bottle had not drained.

Thence to *Redbourn,* where were Players,
None of *Rofcius* active Heirs:
Prologue crown'd with Wreath of Ivy,
Jetted like an Ape moft lively:
I told them fitting at the * Banquet,
They fhould be canvas'd in a Blanket.

From

Actor.
* Even as in a Ban-a-quet are Difh-es
      of fun-dry ta-aft,

Author.
Even fo is thy Doo-blet too long
      i'th' Wa-aft;
Go mend it, thou Knave, go mend it.

Illinc Stomacho inani
Petii oppidum ✱ Albani,
Ubi tantum fecit vinum,
Dirigentem ad Londinum
Manum *manu cepi mea,*
Ac si socia esset ea.

    Veni Barnet *signo Bursæ,*
Ubi convenissent Ursi,
Propinquanti duo horum
Parum studiosi morum,
Subligacula dente petunt,
Quo posteriora fœtent.

    Veni Highgate, *quo prospexi*
✝ *Urbem perdite quam dilexi,*

                              Hi

✱ Hic *Albanus* erat, tumulum, titulumq; reliquit;
   Albion Albanum vix parit alma parem.

✝ Tot colles *Romæ*, quot funt Spectacula *Trojæ*,
   Quæ septem numero, digna labore tuo
   Ista manet *Trojæ* spectacula: 1 Busta, 2 Gigantes,
    3. Histrio, 4. Dementes, 5 Struthiones, 6 Ursa,
    7. Leones.

From thence with a Stomach empty,
To the Town of * *Albane* went I,
Where with Wine I was so undone,
As the *Hand* which guides to *London :*
In my blind Hand I received,
And her more Acquaintance craved.

Thence to th' *Purse* at *Barnet* known-a,
There the Bears were come to Town-a :
Two rude Hunks, 'tis Truth I tell ye,
Drawing near them, they did smell me :
And like two mishapen Wretches,
Made me, ay me, wrong my Bretches.

Thence to *Highgate*, where I viewed
City I so dearly loved,

And

---

* Here *Alban* was, his Tomb, his Title too ;
" All *Albion* shew me such an *Alban* now.

† Seven Hills there were in *Rome*, and so there be
Seven Sights in *New-Troy* crave our Memory :

  1 Tombs, 2 *Guild-hall* Giants, 3. Stage-plays,
    4. *Bethl'hem* Poor,
  5. Ostrich, 6 Bear-garden, 7. Lyons i'th' Tow'r.

Hic Tyronibus exosum
Hausi **Cornu** *tortuosum,*
Ejus memorans salutem
Cujus caput fit cornutum.

Veni **Holloway,** **Pileum rubrum,**
In cohortem muliebrem,
Me **Adonidem** *vocant omnes*
Meretrices **Babylonis ;**
Tangunt, tingunt, molliunt, mulcent,
At egentem, foris pulsant.

Veni **Islington** *ad* **Leonem,**
Ubi spectans Histrionem
Sociatum cum choraulis,
Dolis immiscentem sales,
Cytharæ repsi in vaginam,
Quod præstigiis dedit finem.

Ægre jam relicto rure,
Securem **Aldermanni-bury**

And th' *Horn of Matriculation*
Drank to th' Fleſhmen of our **Nation**;
To his Memory ſaluted
Whoſe branch'd Head was laſt **cornuted.**

Thence to *Holloway*, *Mother Red-cap*
In a Troop of Trulls I did hap;
Whores of *Babylon* me impalled,
And me their *Adonis* called;
With me toy'd they, buſs'd me, **cull'd me,**
But being needy, out they pull'd **me.**

Thence to *Iſlington* at *Lyon*,
Where a juggling I did 'ſpy one
Nimble with his Mates conſorting,
Mixing Cheating with his ſporting:
Creeping into th' Caſe of's Viol,
Spoild his juggling, made them fly all.

Country left I in a Fury,
To the *Axe* in *Alderm'n-bury*

Firſt

Primo petii, qua exosa
Sentina, Holburni Rosa
Me excepit, ordine tali
Appuli Gryphem Veteris Baily;
Ubi experrectus lecto,
Tres Ciconias *indies specto,*
Quo victurus, donec æstas
Rure curas tollet mœstas;
Festus Faustulus *& festivus,*
Calice vividus, corpore vivus.
Ego etiam & Sodales
Nunc Galerum Cardinalis
Visitantes, vi Minervæ
Bibimus ad Cornua Cervi,
Sed Actæon *anxius horum,*
Luce separat Uxorem.

Sub Sigillo Tubi *fumantis*
Et Thyrsi *flammantis,*
Motu Mulciberi *Naso-flagrantis.*

Firſt arriv'd, that place ſlighted,
I at the *Roſe* in *Holbourn* lighted:
From the *Roſe* in Flaggons ſail I
To the *Griffin* i'th *Old-Baily* :
Where no ſooner do I 'waken
Than to *Three Cranes* I am taken ;
Where I lodge, and am no ſtarter
Till I ſee the Summer Quarter.
Pert is *Fauſtulus*, and pleaſing,
Cup brim-full, and Corpſe in ſeaſon :
Yea, my merry Meats and I too
Oft the *Card'nal's Hat* do flie to,
Where at *Harts-horns* we carouſe it,
As *Minerva* doth infuſe it .
But *Actæon*, ſick o'th' Yellows,
Mews his Wife up from Good-fellows.

Under th' Sign of *Pipe* ſtill fuming,
  And the *Buſh* for ever flaming ;
Mulciber the Motion moving,
  With Noſe-burning Maſter ſhaming.

A Shop

Officina juncta Baccho
Juvenilem fere Tobacco,
Uti libet, *tunc fignata,*
Quæ impreffio nunc mutata,
Uti fiet, *nota certa*
Qua delineatur Charta.

Τέλος, *fine* telis *non* typis.

FINIS PARTIS SECUNDÆ.

A Shop neighbouring near *Iacco*,
Where *Young* vends his *Old Tobacco* ˙
As you like it ; fometimes fealed,
Which Impreffion's fince repealed :
As you make it , he will have it,
And in Chart and Front engrave it :

Harmlefs, but no artlefs End
Cloze I here unto my Friend.

THE END OF THE SECOND PART

F

In ERRATA.

INter Accipitrem & Buteonem,
  Juxta phrasem percommunem,
Spectans ista typis data,
Hæc comperui Errata;
Quæ si corrigas (candide Lector)
Plena coronet pocula Nectar.

  A vertice ad calcem
  Erratis admove falcem.

  Errando, disco.

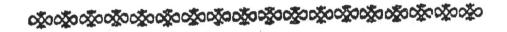

JAm Venus Vinis *reditura* Venis,
  Jam Venus Venis *peritura plenis,*
Nam Venus Venis *patitur serenis,*
  Nectare plenis.

Bar-

Upon the ERRATA's.

BEtwixt *Hawk* and *Buzzard*, O Man,
    After th' Phrafe of Speech fo common,
Having feen this *Journal* at print,
I found thefe *Errata's* in't;
Which if you correct, kind Reader,
Nectar be thy Mufe's feeder.

    From the Head unto the Foot,
    Nought but *Error,* look unto't.

This Obfervation have I found moft true;
Erring, I learn my Errors to fubdue.

NOW *Venus* pure *Veins* are with *Wines*
    inflamed,
Now *Venus* full *Veins* are by *Wines* reftrained:
For *Venus* fwoln *Veins* are by *Morpheus* chained,
    From Folly wained.
        F 2   Bar-

Barnabæ Itinerarium.

PARS III.

Mirtil.

IO Fauftule! *gratulantur*
  Quid te amant & amantur,
Te incolumem rediturum!
Spicta Curia, pone curam,
Narra vias, quas calcafti,
Queis fpirafti, quas fpectafti.

Ne

Barnaby's Journal.

PART III.

Mirtil.

Whoup *Fauſtulus!* all draw nigh thee
    That do love thee, or lov'd by thee,
Joying in thy ſafe returning!
Leave Court Care, and fruitleſs Mourning:
Way th'aſt walked, prithee ſhew it,
Where th'aſt lived, what haſt' viewed.

Ne Ephefios Diana
Fit celebriore fama,
Omnes omnia de te fingunt,
Statuam Pictores pingunt;
Tolle metum, mitte moram,
Fac te clarum viatorem.

Fauftul.

Mitte moram, tolle metum !
Quies me unquam minus lætum
Cum adverfis *agitatum,*
Aut fecundis *tam inflatum*
Vidit, ut mutando morem
Reddant me fuperbiorem.
Afpernarer ego Mundum,
Nifi mundus me jucundum
Bonis Jociis, radiis vitæ
Sociali tinctis fiti
Celebraret, adi, aud,
Et Progreffu meo gaude.

Primo

Not th' *Ephesian Diana*
Is of more renowned Fame-a :
Acting Wonders, all invent thee,
Painters in their Statues paint thee :
Banish Fear, remove Delay Man,
Shew thyself a famous Way-man.

Faustul.

Leave Delay, and be not fearful !
Why! who e'er saw me less chearful ?
When I was by Fortune cuffed,
Or by Fortune's Smiles so puffed,
That I shew'd myself far prouder
Than when she more scornful shew'd her.
For the World, I would not prize her,
Yea, in time I should despise her,
Had she in her no good Fellow,
That would drink till he grew mellow :
Draw near and hear, thou shalt have all,
Hearing, joy in this my Travel.

Primo Die satur vino
Veni Iſlington *à* Londino,
Iter arduum & grove,
Sero tamen superavi,
Acta veſpertina Scena
Siccior eram quam arena.

Veni Kingſland, *terram regis,*
Specioſam cœtu gregis,
Equum ubi fatigantem,
Vix ulterius ſpatiantem,
Nec verberibus nec verbis
Motum, geliais dedi herbis.

Veni Totnam-altam-crucem,
Quo diſceſſi ante lucem,
Hoſpes ſocii parum curet,
Nemo Icaſtulum ſpectaret,

Pretium

First Day, having drank with many,
To *Islington* from *London* came I,
Journey long, and grievous Weather,
Yet the Evening brought me thither;
Having ta'en my Pots by th' Fire,
Summer Sand was never dryer.

Thence to *Kingsland*, where were feeding
Cattle, Sheep, and Mares for breeding;
As I found it, there I feared
That my *Rozinant* was wear'ed:
When he would jog on no faster,
Loose I turn'd him to the Pasture.

Thence to *Totnam-high-crofs* turning,
I departed 'fore next Morning:
Hostess on her Guests so doated,
Stulus was little noted:

Pratum stratum, & Cubile
O piaculum! fit fœnile

  Ut reliqui Crucem altam,
Lento cursu petii Waltham,
In hospitium Oswaldi,
Qui mi regiam * Theobaldi,
Monstrat domum, quo conspecto,
Hausi noctem sine lecto.

  Veni Hoddesden, *stabant foris*
Chartis pictis Impostores,
Queis deceptis, notis causis,
Ante Eirenarcham *pacis*
Eos duxi, ut me videt,
Laudat eos, me deridet.

Ven

---

    * *De augustissima Domo Theobaldi.*

O Domus augustæ radiantia limina nostræ!
An vestrum est Mundi lumine clausa mori?
Regio quo Sponsi pietas dedit oscula Sponsæ,
Et spirare Sabæ vota suprema sua!

To an Hay-loft I was led in,
Boards my Bed, and Straw my Bedding.

Having thus left *High-cross* early,
I to *Waltham* travel'd fairly,
To the Hospital of *Oswald*,
And that Princely Seat of * *The'bald* ;
There all Night I drank old Sack-a,
With my Bed upon my Back-a.

Thence to *Hoddesden*, where stood watching
Cheats who liv'd by Coney-catching :
False Cards brought me, with them play'd I,
Dear for their Acquaintance paid I.
'Fore a Justice they appeared,
Them he praised, me he jeered.

Thence

---

* *On the King's House at* Tibbals.

This Seat, this Royal Object of the Sight,
Shall it for ever bid the World good-night?
Where our preceding Kings enjoy'd such Bliss,
And seal'd their amorous Fancies with a Kiss!

Veni Ware, *ubi belli*
Saltus, situs, & Amwelli
Amnes lenem dantes sonum,
Qui ditarunt Middletonum .
Sunt spectati more miti,
" *O si essent* Aqua vitæ."

Veni Wademill, *ubi rite*
Pleno cyatho dempta siti,
Quidam clamitant jocosè,
Me spectantes otiose,
Co-ementem hæc flagella,
" *Ubi Equus? ubi Sella?*"

Veni Puckeridge, *eo ventum*
Mendicantes fere centum
Me præcingunt; dixi verum,
" *Quod pauperior illis eram,*"
Quo responso, mente una
Me relinquunt cum fortuna.

Ve

Thence to *Ware*, where mazy *Amwel*
Mildly cuts the Southern Chanel;
Rivers streaming, Banks resounding,
Middleton with Wealth abounding.
Mightily did these delight me;
" O, I wish'd them *Aqua vitæ*."

Thence to *Wademill*, where I rest me
For a Pot, for I was thirsty;
On me cry'd they, and did hout me,
And like Beetles flock'd about me.
" Buy a Whip, Sir ! No, a Ladle."
Where's your Horse, Sir ? where your Saddle ?

Thence at *Puckbridge* I reposed,
Hundred Beggars me inclosed.
" Beggars, quoth I, you are many,
" But the poorest of you am I;"
They no more did me importune,
Leaving me unto my Fortune.

Thence

Veni Buntingford, *ad senilem*
Hospitem & juvenilem
Conjugem, quæ scit affari
Placide, lepide osculari,
Area florida, frutice suavis,
Ubi minurizat avis

Veni Royston, *ibi seges,*
Prata, sata, niveæ greges,
Ubi pedes pii Regis,
Hinc evolvens * Fati *æges,*
Mihi dixi : Quid te pejus,
Ista legens, male deges ?

Veni Caxton, *paupere tecto,*
Sed pauperiore lecto :
Quidam habent me suspectum,
Esse maculis infectum

                                    Pestis,

---

* Pascua, prata, canes, viridaria, flumina, saltus,
   Otia regis erant, rege sed ista ruent.

Thence to *Buntingford* right trusty,
Bed-rid Host, but Hostess lusty;
That can chat and chirp it neatly,
And in secret kiss you sweetly;
Here are Arbours decked gaily,
Where the *Buntin* warbles daily.

Thence to *Royston*, there Grass groweth,
Medes, Flocks, Fields, the Plowman soweth;
Where a pious Prince frequented,
Which observing, this I vented:
" Since all Flesh to * Fate's a Debtor,
" Restless Wretch, why liv'st no better?"

Thence to *Caxston*, I was led in
To a poor House, poorer Bedding:
Some there were had me suspected,
That with Plague I was infected;

So

---

* Fields, Floods, Wastes, Woods, Deer, Dogs with
well-tune'd Cry,
Are Sports for Kings, yet Kings with these must die.

Pestis, unde exui vestem,
Vocans Hospitem in testem.

Veni Cambridge, *prope* Vitem,
Ubi Musæ *satiant sitim ;*
Sicut Muscæ circa fimum,
Aut scintillæ in Caminum,
Me clauserunt iuxta murum,
Denegantes rediturum.
Media-Nocte siccior essem,
Ac si nunquam ebibissem,
Sed pudore parum motus,
Hinc discessi semi-potus.
Luci, loci paludosi,
Sed Scholares *speciosi.*

Veni * Godmanchester, *ubi*
Ut Ixion *captus nube,*

Sit

---

* Quercus anilis erat, tamen eminus oppida spectat,
Stirpe viam monstrat, plumea fronde tegit.

So as I ſtark-naked drew me,
Calling th' Hoſteſs ſtrait to view me.

Thence to *Cambridge*, where the *Muſes*
Haunt the *Vine-buſh*, as their Uſe is,
Like Sparks up a Chimney warming,
Or Flies near a Dunghill ſwarming,
In a Ring they did incloſe me,
Vowing they would never loſe me.
'Bout Midnight for Drink I call, Sir,
As I had drank nothing at all, Sir:
But all this did little ſhame me,
Tipſy went I, tipſy came I·
Grounds, Greens, Groves are wet and homely,
But the Scholars wondrous comely.

Thence to * *Godmancheſter*, by one
With a Cloud, as was *Ixion*,

G   Was

Sic elusus à puella,
Cujus labra erant mella,
Lectum se adire vellet,
Spondet, sponsum sed sefellit.

Veni Huntington, *ubi cella*
Facto pacto cum puella,
Hospes *me suspectum habens,*
Et in cellam tacite labens ,
Quo audito, vertens rotam,
Pinxi memet peraegrotum.

Veni Harrington, *bonum omen* [1]
Vere amans illud nomen,
Harringtoni *dedi* nummum,
Et fortunæ penè summum,
Indigenti postulanti,
Benedictionem danti.

Veni Stonegatehole *nefandum.*
Ubi contigit memorandum.

Quidam.

Was I gull'd; fhe had no fellow,
Her foft Lips were moift and mellow;
All Night vow'd fhe to lie by me.
But the Giglet came not nigh me.

    Thence to *Huntington*, in a Cellar.
With a Wench was there a Dweller;
I did bargain, but fufpected
By the Hoft, who her affected;
Down the Stairs he hurried quickly,
While I made me too too fickly.

    Thence to *Harrington*, be it fpoken!
For Name-fake I gave a Token
To a Beggar that did crave it,
And as cheerfully receive it;
More he need not me importune,
For 'twas th' utmoft of my Fortune.

Thence to *Stonegatehole*, I'll tell here
Of a Story that befel there;

One

Quidam Servus Atturnati
Vultu pellicis delicatæ
Captus, intrat nemus mere.
Ut coiret muliere.
Mox è dumo latro repit,
Improvisum eum cepit,
Manticam vertit, mœchum vicit,
Et post Herum nudum misit :
Manibus vinctis Sellæ locat,
Hinnit Equus, Servus vocat.
Cogitemus Attornatum
Suspicantem hunc armatum,
Properantem deprædari,
Uti strenuè calcari .
Currit Herus, metu teste,
Currit Servus sine veste.

Psallens * Sautry, *tumulum veni,*
Sacerdotis locum pœnæ,

Ubi

---

* Urna Sacellani viventis Imago sepulti,
  Quique aliis renuit busta, sepultus erat,
Egregium illud *Sautry* Sacrarium Sacerdotis a-
vari retinuit memoriam.

One who ferved an Attorney,
Ta'en with Beauty in his Journey,
Seeing a Coppice, haftens thither,
Purpofely to wanton with her.
As thefe privately conferred,
A Rover took him unprepared,
Search'd his Portmantua, bound him fafter,
And fent him naked to his Mafter:
Set on's Saddle with Hands ty'd,
Th' Horfe he neyed, Man he cry'd
Th' Attorney, when he had difcerned
One, he thought, behind him, armed
In *white Armour*, ftoutly ftir'd him,
For his Jade, he keenly fpur'd him,
Both run one Courfe to catch a Gudgeon,
This nak'd that frighted to his Lodging

Singing along down * *Sautry* Laning,
I faw a Tomb one had been lain in;

* Here of the Wip a covetous Prieft did lick;
  Who would not bury th' dead, was buried quick.
  Nothing more memorable than that Chapel of
Sautry, retaingng ftill with her that covetous
Prieft's Memory.

Ubi Ransford *jus feciſſet,*
Et Paſtorem *condidiſſet ;*
Vidi, ridi, & avari
Rogo rogos ſic tractari.

　Veni ad Collegium purum,
Cujus habent multi curam ;
Perhumanos narrant mores
Patres, Fratres & Sorores :
Unum tenent, una tendunt,
Omnes omnia Sacris *vendunt.*
An ſint iſti corde puro,
Parum ſcie, minus curo ;
Si ſint, non ſunt Hypocritæ
Orbe melioris vitæ
Cellam, Scholam & Sacellum
Pulchra vidi ſupra Stellam.

　Veni Stilton, *iento more,*
Sine fronde, ſine flore,

And enquiring, one did tell it,
'Twas where *Rainsford* bury'd th' *Prelate*:
I faw, I fmil'd, and could permit it,
Greedy Priefts might fo be fitted.

To th' *Newfounded College* came I,
Commended to the Care of many;
Bounteous are they, kind and loving,
Doing whatfoe'er's behoving
Thefe hold and walk together wholly,
And ftate their Lands on Ufes holy.
Whether pure thefe are, or are not,
As I know not, fo I care not,
But if they be diffembling Brothers,
Their Life furpaffeth many others
See but their Cell, School, and their Temple,
You'll fay the Stars were their Example.

Thence to *Stilton*, flowly paced,
With no Bloom nor Bloffom graced;

With

Sine prunis, sine pomis,
Uti senex sine comis,
Calva tellus, sed benignum
Monstrat viatori signum.

Veni Wansforth-brigs, *immanem*
Vidi amnem, alnum, anum ;
Amnem latum, anum lautam,
Comptam, cultam, castam, cautam ;
Portas, Hortos speciosos,
Portus, saltus spatiosos.

Sed scribentem digitum Dei
Spectans MISERERE MEI,
Atriis, angulis, confestim
Evitandi cura pestem,
Fugi, mori licet natus,
Nondum mori sum paratus.

Inde prato peramœni
Dormiens temulenter fœn.,

Rivus

With no Plumbs nor Apples ſtored,
But bald, like an old Man's Forehead;
Yet with Inns ſo well provided,
Gueſts are pleas'd when they have try'd it.

Thence to *Wansforth-brigs*, a River
And a Wife will live for ever.
River broad, an old Wife jolly,
Comely, ſeemly, free from Folly·
Gates and Gardens neatly gracious,
Ports, and Parks, and Paſtures ſpacious.

Seeing there, as did become me,
Written, LORD HAVE MERCY ON ME,
On the Portals, I departed,
Leſt I ſhould have ſorer ſmarted.
Tho' from Death none may be ſpared,
I to die was ſcarce prepared.

On a Hay-cock ſleeping ſoundly,
Th' River roſe and took me roundly

Down

Rivus surgit & me capit,
Et in flumen alte rapit ;
Quorsum ? clamant ; Nuper erro
A Wansforth-brigs in Anglo-terra.

Veni * Burleigh, *licet Bruma,*
Sunt fornaces sine fumo,
Promptuaria sine promo,
Clara porta, clausa domo ;
† *O Camini sine foco,*
Et Culinæ sine Coquo !
Clamans, domum ô inanem !
Resonabat ‡ Echo, famem ;
Quinam habitant intra muros ?
Respirabat Echo, mures ;
Ditis omen, nomen habe ,
Echo respondebat, Abi.

Veni

---

* Ista domus fit Dasypodis dumus.

Statiu.

† ———Hederæque trophæa camini

‡ ———Custos Domus Echo relicta

Down the Current : People cry'd,
Sleeping down the Stream I hy'd :
Where away, quoth they, *from Greenland ?*
No ; from Wansforth-brigs in England.

Thence to * *Burleigh*, though 'twas Winter,
No Fire did the Chimney enter,
Buttries without Butlers guarded,
Stately Gates were double-warded ;
Hoary † Chimneys without Smoak too,
Hungry Kitchins without Cook too.
Hallowing aloud, O empty Wonder !
‡ *Echo* strait refounded, *Hunger.*
Who inhabits this vaft Brick-houfe ?
Echo made reply, *The Titmoufe :*
Ominous Cell ! No Drudge at home, Sir ?
Echo anfwer made, *Be gone, Sir.*

Thence

---

* This Houfe is the Levarets Bufh.

† Ivy the Chimney's Trophy.

‡ *Echo*'s the Keeper of a forlorn Houfe.

Veni * Stamford, *ubi bene*
Omnis generis crumenæ
Sunt venales, sed in summo
Sunt crumenæ sine nummo;
Plures non in me reptantes,
Quam sunt ibi mendicantes.

Licet curæ premant charæ,
Veni in † Foramen Saræ;
Proca semel succi plena,
Lauta, læta, & serena,
At venusta fit vetusta,
Mundo gravis & onusta.
Saræ antrum *ut intrassem,*
Et ampullas ‡ *gurgitassem,*

In

---

* Quo Schola ? quo Præses ? Comites ? Academica
    sedes ?
    In loculos literas transposuere suas

† Sileni Antrum, eo enim nomine egregie notum.

   ‡ Exiccassem.

Thence to ancient * *Stamford* came I,
Where are pencele∫s Pur∫es many ;
Neatly wrought as doth become, them,
Le∫s Gold in them than is on them :
Clawbacks more do not a∫∫ail me
Than are Beggars ∫warming daily.

Tho' my Cares were great and many,
To the † *Hole of Sarah* came I,
Once a *Bona-roba*, tru∫t me,
Tho' now Buttock-∫hrank and ru∫ty ;
But tho' Nervy-Oil, and fat-a,
Her I caught by you know what-a,
Having boldly thus adventur'd,
And my *Sara*'s Socket enter'd,

Her

---

* Where by thy Ma∫ters ? Fellows ? Scholars ?
    Bur∫ers ?
    O *Stamford* ! to thy ∫hame, they're all turn'd
    Pur∫ers.

† The Drunkard's Cave, for ∫o it mu∫t be call'd,
    Where many Malt-worms have been ∫oundly
    maul'd

In amore Sara *certo,*
Ore basia dat aperto ;
Sæpe sedet, quando surgit
Cyathum propinare urget.

    Veni Witham, *audiens illam*
Propter lubricam anguillam
Vere claram nixus ramo
Cæpi expiscari hamo ;
Et ingentem capians unam.
Præceps trahor in * *lacunam.*

    Veni † Grantham *mihi gratam,*
Inclytè Pyramidatam,
Ibi Pastor cum Uxore
Coeundi utens more,

                               De

---

* Littora Mæandri sunt anxia limina Lethi,
    Fluctus ubi curæ, ripa memento mori.

† Hinc canimus mirum ! non protulit Insula Spiram,
    Talem nec notam vidimus Orbe cotem.

Her I fued, fuited, forted,
Buffed, bouzed, fneezed, fnorted.
Often fate fhe, when fhe got up,
All her Phrafe was, "Drink the Pot up.

Thence to *Witham*, having read there,
That the fatteft Eel was bred there;
Purpofing fome to entangle,
Forth I went and took an Angel;
Where an huge one having hooked,
* By her headlong was I dooked.

Thence to † *Grantham* I retired,
Famous for a Spire afpiring,
There a Paftor with his Sweeting
In a Chamber clofely meeting,

In

---

* *Mæander*'s Shores to *Lethe*'s Shadows tend,
Where Waves, found Cares, and Banks imply our
End,

† I may compare this Town, and be no Lyer,
With any Shire, for Whetftones and a Spire.

De cubiculo defcendit,
Quia papa *ibi pendet.*
Oppidani timent clari
Paulo *Spiram afportari,*
Sciffitantes (valde mirum)
Ubi præparent papyrum,
Qua † *maturius implicetur,*
Ne portando ‡ *læderetur.*

Veni * Newark, *ubi vivos*
Sperans merfos effe rivis,
Irrui cellam fubamænam,
Generofis vinis plenam.

Donec

---

† Structura   ‡ Penetretur.

* Ulmus arenofis pulcherrima nafcitur oris,
    Arces effufis veftit amœna comis.

Hic Campi virides, quos Trentia flumina rivis
Fæcundare folent, ubera veris habent.
    Hic porrectiore tractu diftenditur Bevaria vallis.
        Valles trinæ & opimæ
        Dapes Infulæ divinæ.

In great Fury out he flung there.
'Caufe a Popifh Picture hung there.
Here the Townfmen are amated,
That there Spire fhould be tranflated
Unto *Paul*'s, and great's there Labour,
How to purchafe fo much Paper
To enwrap it, as is fitting,
To fecure their Spire from fplitting.

Thence to ⁂ *Newark*, I lood-furrounded,
Where I hoping moft were drowned,
Hand to Hand I ftraitways fhored
To a Cellar richly ftored

H   Till

---

* A fandy Plat a fhady Elm receives,
   Which cloaths thofe Turrets with her fhilken
      Leaves

Here all-along lies *Bever*'s fpacious Vale,
Near which the Streams of fruitful *Trent* do fall

         Valleys there fo fruitful be
         They're the Wealth of *Britain*

Donec Lictor *intrans cellam,*
Me conduxit ad flagellum.

 Veni Tuxworth *fitam luto,*
Ubi viatores (puto)
Viam viscum effe credunt,
Sedes Syrtes ubi fedent ;
Thyrfus pendet, diu pendit,
Bonum Vinum raro vendit,

 Veni Retfrod, *Pifces edi,*
Et adagio locum dedi,
Cæpi ftatim propinare,
Ut pifciculi natare
Difcant meo corpore vivo,
Sicuti natarunt rivo.

 Veni Scrubie, *Deus bone !*
Cum Paftore & Latrone
Egi diem, fregi noctem,
Latro me feciffet doctum :

Et

Till fufpected for a Pick-lock,
Th' Beadle led me to the Whip-ftock.

Thence to *Tuxworth*, in the Clay there,
Where poor Travellers find fuch Way there,
Ways like Bird-lime feem to fhew them,
Seats are Syrts to fuch as know them;
Th' Ivy hangs there, long has't hung there,
Wine it never vended ftrong there.

Thence to *Retford*, Fifh I fed on,
And to th' Adage I had red on;
With Caroufes I did trim me,
That my Fifh might fwim within me
As they had done being living
And i'th' River nimbly diving.

Thence to *Scrubie*, O my Maker!
With a *Paftor* and a *Taker*
Day I fpent, I Night divided,
Thief did make me well provided:

Et nollem affidere,
Ne propinquior effes peræ.

Veni Bautree, *angiportam,*
In dumetis vidi Scortam,
Geftu levem, lumine vivam,
Vultu lætam, & lafcivam;
Sed inflixi carni pænam,
Timens mifere crumenam.

Veni † Doncafter, *fed* Levitam
Audiens finiffe vitam,
Sprevi Venerem, *fprevi* Vinum,
Perdite quæ dilexi primum.
Nam cum Venus *infenefcit,*
In me carnis vim compefcit.

Nefcit-

---

† Major Caufidico quo gratior effet amico,
　　In comitem lento tramite jungit equo.
　　Caufidicus renuit, renuente, Patibula, dixit,
　　Commonftrabo tibi, *Cauf.* Tuque moreris ibi.

My poor Scrip caus'd me to fear him,
All Night long I came not near him.

Thence to *Bautree*, as I came there,
From the Bushes near the Lane, there
Rush'd a Tweak in Gesture flanting,
With a leering Eye, and wanton:
But my Flesh I did subdue it,
Fearing left my Purse should rue it.

Thence to † *Doncaster*, where reported
Lively *Levite* was departed
Love I loath'd, and spritely Wine too,
Which I dearly lov'd some time too,
For when youthful *Venus* rageth,
She my fleshly Force aswageth.

H 3   Thirst

---

† That Courtesie might a Courtesie enforce,
The May'r would bring the Lawyer to his Horse
You shall not, quoth the Lawyer. M *Now I swear*
I'll to the Gallows go   L. *I'll have you there*
Might not this May'r (for Wit a second Pale As)
Have ram'd the *Town-end* full as well as *Gallows*

Nescit sitis artem modi,
Puteum Roberti Hoodi
Veni, & liquente vena
Vincto * *catino catena,*
Tollens sitim, parcum odi,
Solvens obolum Custodi.

   Veni † Wentbridge, *ubi plagæ*
Terræ, maris, vivunt sagæ,
Vultu torto & anili,
Et conditione vili
His infernæ manent sedes,
Quæ cum inferis ineunt fœda.

   Veni Ferrybrig, *vietus,*
Pede lassus, mente lætus,

                                        Ut

---

* Viventes venæ, Spinæ, catinusque catenæ,
  Sunt *Robin Hoodi* nota trophæa sui,

† Rupæ cavedia struxit inedia,
  Queis oscitanter latuit accedia.

Thirst knows neither Mean nor Measure,
Robin Hood's Well was my Treasure;
In a common * Dish enchained,
I my furious Thirst restrained:
And because I drank the deeper,
I paid two Farthings to the Keeper.

Thence to † *Wentbridg*, where vile Wretches,
Hideous Hags and odious Witches,
Writhen Count'nance, and mis-shapen,
Are by some foul *Bugbear* taken:
These infernal Seats inherit,
Who contract with such a Spirit.

Thence to *Ferrybrig*, sore wearied,
Surfoot, but in Spirit cheered

H 4   I no

---

* A Well, Thorn, Dish, hung in an Iron Chain
For Monuments of *Robin Hood* remain.

† In a Rock Want built her Booth,
Where no Creature dwells but Sloth

Ue guſtaſſem uvam Vini,
Fructum ſalubrem acini :
Sævior factus ſum quam Aper,
Licet vini lenis ſapor.

   Veni ＊ Pomfret, *ubi miram*
Arcem, † Anglis *regibus diram,*
Laſeris ‡ *ortu celebrandam,*
Variis geſtis memorandam
Nec in Pomfret *Reper***,*
Quam pauperculus mei***.

   Veni Sherburn *ad amandum,*
Et aciculis ſpectandum,
                          Paſtor

---

* Hic repetunt ortum triſtiſſima funera Regum,
   Quæ lachrymas oculis excuſſere meis

† Regibus Anglorum dedit arx tua dira ruinam;
   Hoc titulo fatum cerne   . . tuum

‡ Latius in rupem Laſer eſt ſita dulcis arentem,
   Veſte nova Veris floribus aucta novis.

I no fooner the Grape tafted
But my Melancholy wafted
Never was wild Boar more fellifh,
Tho' the Wine did finally relifh.

Thence to * *Pomfret*, as long fince is,
Fatal to our † *Englifh* Princes,
For the choiceft ‡ *Liquorice* crowned,
And for fundry Acts renowned
A *Loule* in *Pomfret* is not furer
Than the Poet thro' Sloth fecurer

Thence to *Sherium*, dearly loved,
And for Pinners well approved.

Cherry-

---

* The Tragick State of *Englifh* Kings flood here
  Which to their Urns pays Tribute with a Tear,

† Here flood that fatal Theatre of Kings,
  Which for Revenge mounts up with airy Wings

‡ Here *Liquorice* grows upon their mellow'd Bunks,
  Decking the Spring with her delicious Plants.

Paſtor decimas ceraſorum
Quærit plus quam animorum :
Certe neſcio utrum mores,
An fortunæ meliores.

   Veni Bramham,, *eo ventus,*
Vidi Pedites currentes ;
Quidam auribus fuſurrat,
" *Crede* Fauſtule, *hic præcurret,*
" *Nam probantur . Qui narratur*
Pejor, melior auſpicatur.

   Veni Tadcaſter, *ubi pontem*
Sine flumine, prælucentem,
Plateas fractas, & aſtantes
Omni loco mendicantes
Spectans, illinc divagatei,
Ne cum illis numerarer.

   Veni Eboracum, *flore*
Juventutis eum Textore

                      , *Fruen*

Cherry-Tenths the Paftor aimeth,
More than th' Souls which he reclaimeth.
In an Equipage conforting,
Are their Manners and their Fortune.

    Thence to *Bramham*, thither coming,
I faw too Footmen ftript for running
One faid, "the Match was made to cheat 'em
"Truft me, *Fauftulus*, *This* will beat 'em;
"For we've try'd 'em; but that Courfer
He priz'd better, prov'd the worfer.

    Thence to *Tadcafter*, where ftood reared
A fair Bridge, no Flood appeared:
Broken Pavements, Beggars waiting,
Nothing more than Labour hating;
But with fpeed I faftned from them,
Left I fhould be thought one of them.

Thence to *York*, frefh Youth enjoying,
With a wanton *Weaver* toying:

                Husband

Fruens, conjux statim venit,
" *Lupum vero auribus tenet;*
Ille clamat aperire,
Ille negat exaudire.

Sic ingreßus mihi datur,
Cum Textori *denegatur;*
Qui dum voce importunè
Strepit, matulam urinæ
Sentit; sapienter tacet,
Dum Betricia *mecum jacet,*

Ibi Tibicen apprehensus,
Judicatus & suspensus,
Plaustro coaptato furi,
Ubi Tibia, *clamant pueri?*
Nunquam ludes amplius Billie;
At nescitis, *inquit ille.*
Quod contigerit memet teste,
Nam abscißa jugulo reste,
Ut in foßam Furcifer vexit,
Semi-mortuus resurrexit:

Husband suddenly appears too,
" Catching the *Wolf* by th' Ears too :
He cries, *Open, something fears him :*
But th' deaf *Adder* never hears him.

Thus my Entrance was descried,
While the *Weaver* was denied ;
Who as he fumed, fret, and frowned,
With a Chamber-pot was crowned :
Wisely silent, he ne'er grudged
That his *Betty* with me lodged.

A Piper being here committed,
Guilty found, condemn'd, and titted ;
As he was to *Knavesmyre* going,
This Day, quoth Boys, *will spoil thy Blowing ;*
From thy Pipe th'art now departing ;
Wags, quoth th' Piper, *you're not certain*
All which happen'd to our Wonder,
For the Halter cut asunder,
As one of all Life deprived,
Being bury'd, he revived :

And

Arce reducem occludit,
Ubi va'et, vivit, ludit.

Veni Towlerton, *Stadiodromi*
Retinentes spem coronæ,
Ducunt equos ea die
Juxta tramitem notæ viæ,
Sequens autem solitam venam,
Sprevi primum & postremum.

Veni Helperby *desolatum,*
Igne nuper concrematum,
Ne taberna fit intacta,
Non in cineres redacta ;
Quo discessi ocyor Euro,
Restinguendi sitim cura.

Veni * Topcliff, *musicam vocans.*
Et decoro ordine locans,

Ut

---

* Labentes rivi refonant fub vertice clivi,
    Quæ titulum villæ primo dedere tuæ.
                Alias,
    Infra fitum Rivi faliunt fub acumine clivi,
    Quo fedes civi fplendida, nulla nivi.

And there lives, and plays his Meafure,
Holding Hanging but a Pleafure.

Thence to *Towlerton*, where thofe Stagers,
Or Horfe-courfers run for Wagers :
Near to the Highway the Courfe is,
Where they ride and run their Horfes :
But ftill on our Journey went we,
Firft or *Laft* did 'like content me.

Thence to *Helperby* I turned,
Defolate and lately burned :
Not a Taphoufe there but mourned,
Being all to Afhes turned ;
Whence I fwiftly did remove me.
For Thirft-fake, as did behove me.

Thence to * *Topcliff*, Mufick call'd I,
In no comely Pofture fail'd I ;

But

---

* *Topcliff* from tops of Cliffs firft took her Name,
And her Cliff-mounted Seat confirms the fame :
Where Streams with curled Windings overflown,
Beftow a Native Beauty on the Town.

Ut expectant hi mercedem,
Tacitè subtraxi pedem;
Parum habui quod experdam,
Linquens eos ad solvendum

*Veni * Thyrske, Thyrsis hortum,*
Ubi Phyllis floribus sportam
Instruit, at nihil horum
Nec pastorem, neque florem
Ego curo, Bacchum specto
Horto, campo, foro, tecto.

Veni Alerton, ubi oves,
Tauri, vaccæ, vituli, boves,
Aliaque Campi pecora
Oppidana erant decora ·

                                      Forum

---

* Thyrsis oves pascens per apricæ pascua vallis,
   Prima dedit Thyrsco nomina nota suo.

   Sycamori gelidis Tityrus umbris
   Discumbens, Phyllidi Serta paravit,
   Et niveas greges gramine pavit.

But when thefe expected Wages,
To themfelves I left my Pages;
Small being th' Court'fy I could fhew them,
Th' Reck'ning I commended to them.

Thence to * *Thyrfke*, rich *Thyrfis* Cafket,
Where fair *Phyllis* fills her Bafket
With choice Flowers, but thefe be vain things,
I efteem no Flowers, nor Swainlings;
In *Bacchus* Yard, Field, Booth, or Cottage,
I love nought like his cold Pottage.

Thence to *Alerton*, rank'd in Battel,
Sheep, Kine, Oxen, other Cattel;
As I fortun'd to pafs by there,
Were the Town's beft beautifier

I   Fair

---

* Here *Thyrfis* fed his Lamblins on the Plain;
So *Thyrfke* from *Thyrfis* took her ancient Name
Here *Tityrus* and *Phyllis* made them Bowers,
Of tender Ofiers, fweet-breath'd Sycamours.

Forum fuit jumentorum,
Mihi autem cella forum.

Veni Smeton, *perexofum*
Collem *quem* pediculofum
Vulgo vocant, tamen mirè
Mœchæ folent lafcivire,
Ad alendum debilem ftatum,
Aut tegendam nuditatem.

Veni * Nafham, Dei donum,
In Cœnobiarchæ domum;
Uberem vallem, falubrem venam,
Curfu fluminis amœnam,
Lætam fylvis & frondofam,
Heræ vultu fpeciofam.

Veni:

---

* ¹ tora Latifris, gemmarunt germina gemmis,
Murenulis conchæ, muricibufque comæ.

Fair for Beasts at that time fell there,
But I made my Fare the Cellar.

Thence to *Smeton* I assailed,
Lousy Hill, for so they call it;
Where were dainty Ducks, and jant ones,
Wenches that could play the wantons;
Which they practice, Truth I'll tell ye,
For Relief of Back and Belly.

Thence to * *Nesham*, now translated,
Once a *Nunnery* dedicated:
Valleys smiling, Bottoms pleasing,
Streaming Rivers never ceasing;
Deck'd with tufty Woods and shady,
Graced by a lovely Lady

I 2   Thence

---

* Where Shores yield Lentisks, Branches pearled
   Gems,
   There Lamprels Shells, their Rocks soft mossy
   Stems.

Veni Darlington, *prope vicum*
Conjugem duxi peramicam,
Nuptus celebrantur festa,
Nulla admittuntur mœsta;
Potula noctis dant progressum,
Ac si nondum nuptus essem.

Veni * Richmond, *sed amicos*
Generosos & antiquos,
Nobiles socios, sortis miræ,
Cum nequissem invenire,
Sepelire curas ibi,
Tota nocte mecum bibi.

Pœna sequi solet culpam,
Veni Redmeere *ad* Subulcum,

Iba

---

* Nomen habes Mundi, nec erit fine jure, fecundi,
Namque fitus titulum comprobat ipfe tuum.

Thence to *Darlington*, where I bouſed
Till at laſt I was eſpouſed :
Marriage Feaſt and all prepared,
Not a Fig for th' World I cared ;
All Night long by th' Pot I tarry'd,
As if I had ne'er been marry'd.

Thence to * *Richmond*, heavy Sentence !
There were none of my Acquaintance.
All my noble Comrades gone were,
Of them all I found not one there ;
But leſt Care ſhould make me ſicker,
I did bury Care in Liquor.

Penance chac'd that Crime of mine hard,
Thence to *Redmeere*, to a Swine-herd

I 3   Came

---

* From a *Rich Mound* thy Appellation came,
And thy rich Seat proves it a proper Name.

Ilia menfæ fert porcina,
Prifca nimis inteftina,
Quæ ni calices abluiffent,
Adhuc gurgite inhæfiffent.

Veni Carperbie peravarum.
Cœtu frequens, victu carum ;
Septem Solidorum cœna
Reddit levior crumena :
Nummo citius haurieris,
Quam liquore ebrieris.

Veni Wenchly, valle fitum,
Prifca vetuftate tritum,
Amat tamen propinare
Paftor cum agnellis charè,
Quo effafcinati more,
Dormiunt Agni cum Paftore.

Veni Middlam, ubi arcem
Vidi, & bibentes fparfim

Bonos

Came I, where they nothing plac'd me
But a Swine's Gut that was nasty;
Had I not then wash'd my Liver,
In my Guts't had stuck for ever.

Thence to *Carperby*, very greedy,
Conforts frequent, Victuals needy:
After Supper they so toss'd me,
As seven Shillings there it cost me:
Soon may one of Coin be soaked,
Yet for want of Liquor choaked.

Thence to *Wenchly*, Valley-seated,
For Antiquity repeated·
Sheep and Shepherd, as one Brother,
Kindly drink to one another,
Till Pot-hardy, light as Feather,
Sheep and Shepherd sleep together.

Thence to *Middlam*, where I viewed
Th' Castle which so stately shewed:

I 4 Down

Bonos focios, quibus junxi,
Et liquorem libere fumpfi;
Æneis licet tincti nafis,
Fuimus cuftodes pacis.

Veni * Ayfcarth, *vertice montis,*
Valles, & amœnos fontes,
Niveas greges, fcopulos rudes,
Campos, karpos, & paludes
Vidi, locum vocant Templum,
Speculantibus exemplum.

Veni Worton, *fericis cincta,*
Sponfa Ducis, ore tincta,
Me ad cœnam blande movet,
Licet me non unquam novit,
Veni, vidi, vifi, lufi,
' *Cornu-copiam optans Duci*

Veni

---

* Gurgite præcipiti fub vertice montis acuti
Specus erat fpinis obfitus, intus aquis.

Down the Stairs, 'tis Truth I tell ye,
To a Knot of brave Boys fell I :
All *Red Nofes*, no Dye deeper,
Yet none but a Peace-keeper,

Thence to * *Ayfcarth*, from a Mountain,
Fruitful Valleys, pleafant Fountain,
Woolly Flocks, Cliffs ?eep and fnowy,
Fields, Fenns, fedgy Rufhes faw I,
Which high Mount is call'd the *Temple*,
For all Profpects an Example

Thence to *Werton*, being lighted,
I was folemnly invited
By a Captain's Wife moft yewly,
Though, I think, fhe never knew me
I came, call'd, cull'd, toy'd, trifled, kiffed.
" Captain cornu-cap d I wifhed.

Thence

---

* Here breaths an arched Cave of antique Stature,
. Clofed above with Thorns, below with Water.

Veni Bainbrig, *ubi palam*
Flumen doferit canalem,
Spectans, uti properarem
Ad Joannem Ancillarem,
Hospitem habui (verè mirum)
Neque fœminam, neque virum.

Veni * Afkrig, *notum Forum,*
Valde tamen indecorum,
Nullum habet Magiftratum,
Oppidanum ferre ftatum ·
Hic pauperrimi textores.
Peragreftes tenent mores.

Veni † Hardraw, *ubi Fames,*
Cautes frugis perinanes ,

Nun-

---

* Clauditur amniculus faliens fornicibus arctis,
     Alluit & villæ mœnia juncta fuæ.

† Labitur alveolis refonantibus amnis amœnus,
     Qui tremula mulcet voce, fopore fovet.

Thence to *Bainbrig*, where the River
From its chanel feems to fever.
To *Maidenly John* I forthwith hafted,
And his beft Provifion tafted·
Th' Hoft I had (a thing not common)
Seemed neither Man nor Woman.

Thence to * *Afkbrig*, Market noted,
But no Handfomenefs about it;
Neither Magiftrate nor Mayor
Ever were elected there·
Here poor People live by Knitting,
To their Trading, breeding fitting

Thence to † *Hardraw*, where', hard Hunger,
Barren *Cliffs* and *Clints* of Wonder;

            Never

---

* A Chanel ftrait confines a Cryftal Spring,
  Wafhing the Walls o'th' Village neighbouring.

† A fhallow Rill, whofe Streams their Current keep,
  With murm'ring Voice and Pace procure fweet
  Sleep.

Nunquam vixit hic Adonis,
Ni sub thalamo Carbonis :
Diversoria sunt obscœna,
Fimo sœda, fumo plena.

Veni Gastile, ubi cellam,
Cellam sitam ad Sacellum
Intrans, bibi Stingo *fortem,*
Habens Lanium in consortem,
Et * *Pastorem parvæ gregis,*
Rudem moris, artis, legis.

Veni † Sedbergh, *sedem quondam*
Lautam, lætam, & jucundam,
Sed mutatur mundus totus,
" *Vix in anno unus potus :*

Ibi

---

* Quota est hora, refert ! Solem speculando respon-
  Ecce Sacerdotes quos tua terra parit !   [der,

† Prospicies Thyrsum sinuosius arte rotundum,
  Organa quo cerebri mersa fuere mei.

Never here *Adonis* lived,
Unless in *Cole*'s Harbour hived :
Inns are nasty, dusty, fusty,
With both Smoke and Rubbish musty.

Thence to *Gastile*, I was drawn in
To an Alehouse near adjoining
To a *Chapel*; I drank *Stingo*
With a *Butcher* and *Domingo*
Th' * *Curate*, who, to my discerning,
Was not guilty of much Learning.

Thence to † *Sedbergh*, sometimes Joy-all,
Gamesome, gladsome, richly royal ;
But those Jolly Boys are sunken,
" Now scarce once a Year one drunken :

There

---

* I ask'd him, What's a-Clock ? he look'd at th' Sun,
  But want of Learning made him answer—Mum.

† Here grows a Bush in artful Mazes round,
  Where th' active Organs of my Brain were
  drown'd.

Ibi propriæ prope lari
Non audebam Vulpinari.

    Veni * Killington, *editum collem,*
Fronde lætiore mollem,
Ibi tamen parum hærens.
Semper altiora sperans,
Hisce dixi longum vale,
Solum repetens natale.

    Veni † Kendall, *ubi status*
Præstans, prudens ‡ *Magistratus,*

                              Publicis

---

* Arboribus gelidam texens Coriarius umbram,
  Æstatem atque Hyemem fronde repelle gravem.

  † Nunc Saturnius appulit annus,
    Major fiet Aldermannus.

There I durſt not well be merry,
Far from Home old Foxes werry.

Thence to * *Killington* I paſſed,
Where an Hill is freely graſſed ;
There I ſtaid not, tho' half-tired,
Higher ſtill my Thoughts aſpired :
Taking Leave of Mountains many,
To my Native Country Came I.

Thence to *Kendall*, pure her State is,
Prudent too her † Magiſtrate is ;

In

---

* Here the retir'd Tanner builds him Bowers
Shrouds him from Summer's Heat, and Winter's
    Showers.

† Now *Saturn's* Year has drench'd down Care,
And made an Alderman a May'r.

Publicis Festis purpuratus,

Ab Elizabetha *datus;*

Hic me juvat habitare,

Propinare & amare.

Inter Barnabæ *Errores,*

Hi mutârunt pi eli mores,

" *Delirans iste Sapiens* Gottam

" *Reddit* Cœtum *propter* Cotem."

Vide Grantham.

FINIS PARTIS TERTIÆ.

In whofe Charter to them granted,
Nothing but a Mayor wanted :
Here it likes me to be dwelling,
Boufing, loving ; Stories telling.

Amongft other Faults in Print,
You fhall find this Error in't :
" Did not the Stage of *Gottam* ftrangely fail,
" Who for a *Whetftone* render'd him a *Whale?*"

See *Grantham.*

THE END OF THE THIRD PART.

Bar-

Barnabæ Itinerarium.

PARS IV.

Mirtil.

O Fauſtule! *dic quo jure*
Spreta Urbe, vivis rure?
Quo tot lepidos conſortes,
Genio fauſtos gurgite fortes,
Reliquiſti, ſocios vitæ,
Gravi laborantes ſiti?

Vale

Barnaby's Journal.

PART IV.

Mirtil.

O *Fauflu'us!* takes't no Pity
　　For the Field to leave the City?
Nor thy Conforts, lively Skinkers,
Witty Wags, and lufty Drinkers;
Lads of Life, who wafh their Liver,
And are dry and thirfty ever?

Wilt

Vale dices tot amicis,
Tot Lyæi vini vicis,
Tot Falerni roscidi cellis,
Tot pelliculis, tot puellis?
Quid te movet, dic sodali,
Urbi longum dicere vale?

Fauſtul.

Quid me movet! *Nonne cernis*
Me tamdiu in Tabernis
Propinaſſe, donec mille
Clamant, Ecce *Fauſtulus* ille,
Qui per Orbem ducens iter,
Titulo *Ebrii* inſignitur!
Qui natali bibit more
Ortu roſeæ ab Auroræ
Uſque veſperam, & pudorem
Vultûs, queſtus & odorem
Sprevit! *audi culpæ pœnam,*
Scenam Fauſtuli *extremam.*

Vale

Wilt thou here no longer tarry
With thefe Boys that love *Canary?*
Wilt thou leave thefe Nectar Trenches,
Dainty Doxies, merry Wenches?
Say, what makes thee change thy Ditty,
Thus to take Farewel o'th' City?

Fauftul.

What is't makes me! Doft' not note it,
How I have i'th' Tavern floated,
Till a Thoufand feek to fhame me,
There goes Fauftulus, fo they name me,
Who thi o' all the World has traced,
And with Stile of Maltworm *graced!*
Who caroufeth to his Breeding,
From Aurora's *Beamlins fpreading*
To th' Evening, and defpifeth
Favour-Thrift, which each Man prizeth!
Now hear *Fauftulus's* Melancholy,
Th' clofing Scene of all his Folly.

Fare-

*V*Ale Banbury, *vale* Brackley,
   Vale Hollow-well, *vale* Hockley,
Vale Daintry, *vale* Leifter,
Vale Chichefter, *vale* Chefter,
Vale Nottingham, *vale* Mans'field,
Vale Wetherby, *vale* Tanfield.

   Vale Aberford, *vale* Bradford,
Vale Toceter, *vale* Stratford,
Vale Prefton, *vale* Euxfton,
Vale Wigan, *vale* Newton,
Vale Warrington, *vale* Budworth,
Vale Kighley, *vale* Cudworth.

   Vale Hoddefden, *vale* Totnam,
Vale Gigglefwick, *vale* Gottam,
Vale Harrington, *vale* Stilton,
Vale Huntington, *vale* Milton,

                         Vale

FArewel *Banbury,* farewel *Brackley,*
   Farewel *Hollow-well,* farewel *Hockley,*
Farewel *Daintry,* farewel *Leiſter,*
Farewel *Chicheſter,* farewel *Cheſter,*
Farewel *Nottingham,* farewel *Mansfield,*
Farewel *Wetherby,* farewel *Tanfield.*

   Farewel *Aberford,* farewel *Bradford,*
Farewel *Toceter,* farewel *Stratford,*
Farewel *Preſton,* farewel *Euxſton,*
Farewel *Wigan,* farewel *Newton,*
Farewel *Warrington,* farewel *Budworth,*
Farewel *Kighley,* farewel *Cudworth.*

   Farewel *Hoddeſden,* farewel *Totnam,*
Farewel *Giggleſwick,* farewel *Gottam,*
Farewel *Harrington,* farewel *Stilton,*
Farewel *Huntington,* farewel *Milton,*

Fare-

Vale Royſton, *vale* Puckeridge,
Vale Caxſton, *vale* Cambridge.   -

Vale Ware, *vale* Wademill,
Vale High-gate, *vale* Gads-hill,
Vale Stamford, *vale* Sautry,
Vale Scrubie, *vale* Bautry,
Vale Caſtrum Subterlinum,
Ubi Vates, *Venus*, *vinum*.

Vale Tauk-hill, *quem conſpexi*,
Lemnia Lydia, *quam dilexi*,
Arduæ viæ quas tranſivi,
Et amiculæ queis coivi,
Faber, Taber, ſociæ lætæ,
Et convivæ vos valete.

Nunc longinquos locos odi,
Vale fons Roberti Hoodi,
Vale Roſington, *vale* Retford,
Et antiqua ſedes Bedford ;

Vial

Farewel *Royston*, farewel *Puckeridge*,
Farewel *Caxston*, farewel *Cambridge*.

Farewel *Ware*, farewel *Wademill*,
Farewel *High-gate*, farewel *Gads-hill*,
Farewel *Stamford*, farewel *Sautry*,
Farewel *Scrubie*, farewel *Bautry*,
Farewel *Castle Underline* too,
Where are Poets, Wenches, Wine too.

Farewel *Tauk-hill*, which I viewed,
Lemnian Lydia, whom I sued ;
Steepy Ways by which I waded,
And those Truggs with which I traded ;
Faber, Taber, pensive never,
Farewel merry Mates for ever.

Now I hate all foreign Places,
Robin Hood's Well, and his Chaces :
Farewel *Rosington*, farewel *Retford*,
And thou antient Seat of *Bedford* ;

Fare-

Vale Dunchurch, Dunstable, Brickhill,
Alban, Barnet, Pimlico, Tickhill.

  Vale Waltham, & Oswaldi
Sedes, situs Theobaldi,
Vale Godmanchester, *ubi*
Mens elusa fuit nube;
Vale Kingsland, Islington, * London,
Quam amavi perdite quondam.

Vale

●——Ista novæ mea mœnia Trojæ.

  Nunc novæ longum valedico Trojæ,
  Læta quæ flori, gravis est senectæ,
  Vina, Picturæ, Veneris facetæ,
      Cuncta valete.

  Sin vero conjux, famuli, sorores,
  Liberi, suaves Laribus lepores
  Confluant, mulcent varios labores
      Cuncta venite.

Farewel *Dunchurch, Dunstable, Brickhill,*
Alban, Barnet, Pimlico, Tickhill.

Farewel *Waltham,* Seat of *Oswald,*
That bright Princely Star of *The'baid :*
Farewel *Godmanchestei,* where I
Was deluded by a Fairy.
Farewel *Kingsland, Islington,* * *London,*
Which I lov'd, and by it undone.

Farewel

---

*——Thefe be my *New Troy*'s dying Elegies.

Now to that *New Troy* bid adieu for ever,
Wine, Venus, Pictures, can alure me never,
Thefe are Youth's Darlings, Age's hoary griever,
Fare ye well ever.

Farewel for ever, fee you will I never,
Yet if Wife, Children, Money hurry thither,
Where we may plant and folace us together,
Welcome for ever.

Vale Buntingford, *ubi fuaves*
Vepres, vites, flores, aves,
Hofpes grata & benigna,
Et amoris præbens figna ;
Alio juvat fpatiari,
Pafci, pati, recreari.

Vale Stone, & Sacellum,
Quod fplendentem habet Stellam,
Vale Haywood, Bruerton, Ridglay,
Litchfield, Coventry, Colefhill, Edglay.
Meredin, Wakefield, & *amœni*
Campi, chori Georgii Greeni.

Vale Clowne, Doncafter, Rothram,
Clapham, Ingleton, Waldon, Clothram,
Witham, Grantham, New-wark, Tuxworth,
Uxbridge, Beconsfield, & Oxforth,
Geniis & ingeniis bonis
Satur, opibus Platonis.

Sprevi

Farewel *Buntingford,* where are Thrushes,
Sweet Briers, shred Vines, private Bushes;
Hostess cheerful, mildly moving,
Giving Tokens of her loving;
I must in another Nation
Take my fill of Recreation.

Farewel precious *Stone* and *Chapel,*
Where *Stella* shines more fresh than th'Apple;
Farewel *Haywood, Bruerton, Ridglay,*
Litchfield, Coventry, Coleshill, Edgway,
Meredin, Wakefield, farewel clean-a
Medes and Mares of *George à Green*-a.

Farewel *Clowne, Doncaster, Rothram,*
Clapham, Ingleton, Waldron, Clothram,
Witham, Grantham, New-wark, Tuxworth,
Uxbridge, Beconsfield, and *Oxforth,*
Richly stor'd (I am no *Gnatho*)
With Wit, Wealth, Worth, Well of *Plato.*

Fare-

Sprevi nunc Textoris *acum,*
Vale, vale Eboracum,
Alio nunc victurus more,
Mutans mores cum * *colore;*
Horreo, proprium colens nidum,
Sacram violare fidem.

Vale Wentbrig, Towlerton, Sherburn,
Ferrybrig. Tadcaster, Helperby, Merburn:
Vale Bairbrig, Askrig, Worton,
Hardraw, Wenchley, Smeton, Burton:
Vale Ayscarth, Carperby, Redmeere,
Gastile, Killington, & Sedbergh.

Armen-

---

* Incessit hyems niveis capillis,
   Incessit hyems gelidis lacertis,
   Nec mea curat carmina Phyllis,
   Urbe relecta rustica vertes

Conspicui vates repetendo Cupidinis æstus,
Spreta canunt lepidis, ut senuere, procis.

Farewel *York*, I muſt forſake thee,
Weaver's Shuttle ſhall not take me:
* Hoary Hairs are come upon me,
Youthful Pranks will not become me;
Th' Bed to which I'm reconciled
Shall be by me ne'er defiled.

Farewel *Wentbrig, Towlerton, Sherburn,*
Ferry-brig, Tadcaſter, Helperby, Merburn;
Farewel *Bainbrig, Aſkrig, Worton,*
Hardraw, Wenchley, Smeton, Burton;
Farewel *Ayſcarth, Carperby, Redmeer,*
Gaſtile, Killington, and *Sedbergh.*

I am

---

* Winter has now behoar'd my Hairs,
  Benumb'd my Joints and Sinews to;
Phyllis for Verſes little Cares,
  Leave City then, to th' Country go.

Poets, when they have writ of Love their fill,
Grown old, are ſcorn'd, tho' Fancy crown their
  Quill.

Armentarius jam sum factus,
Rure manens incoactus,
Suavis odor lucri tenet,
Parum curo unde venit,
Campo, choro, tecto, thoro,
Caula, cella, sylva, foro.

Equestria Fora.

Veni Malton, artem laudo,
Vendens Equum sine cauda,
Morbidum, mancum, claudum, cecum,
Forte si maneret mecum,
Probo, vendo, pretium datur,
Quid si statim moriatur.

Ad forensem Rippon, tendo,
Equi si sint cari, vendo,
Si minore pretio dempti,
Equi à me erunt empti,

"*Ut*

I am now become a Drover,
Country Liver, Country Lover;
Smell of Gain my Senfe benumbeth,
Little care I whence it cometh,
Be't from Camp, Choir, Cottage, Carpet,
Field, Fold, Cellar, Foreft, Market.

Horfe Fairs.

To *Malton* come I, praifing th' Sale, Sir,
Of an Horfe without a Tail, Sir,
Be he maim'd, lam'd, blind, difeafed,
If I fell him, I'm well pleafed;
Should this Kephal die next morrow,
I partake not in the Sorrow.

Then to *Rippon*, I appear there
To fell Horfes if they're dear there;
If they're cheap, I ufe to buy them,
And i'th' Country profit by them;

L

" Where

"*Ut alacrior fiat ille,*
"*Ilia mordicant anguillæ.*

Septentrionalia Fora.

Veni Pomfret, *uberem venam,*
* *Virgis laserpitiis plenam.*

Veni Topcliff *cum sodali,*
Non ad Vinum sed venale.

Veni Thyrsk *ubi Boves*
Sunt venales pinguiores.

Veni Alerton *lœtam, latam,*
Mercatori perquam gratam,
In utiliorem actum,
Eligo locum pecori aptum.

Veni

---

* Virgulta Laseris florent amœnula.
In hac Angelica latius Insula.
Vide lib. 3. stanz. 48.

" Where to quicken 'em, I'll tell ye,
" I put quick Eels into their Belly.

Northern Fairs.

Thence to *Pomfret*, freshly flowred,
And with * Rods of Liquorice stored.

Thence to *Topcliff* with my Fellow,
Not to bouze Wine, but to sell low

Thence to *Thyrsk*, where Bullocks grazed
Are for Sale i'th Market placed

Thence to *Alerton*, cheerful, fruitful,
To the Seller very grateful ;
There to chufe a Place, I'm chariest,
Where my Beasts may shew the fairest,
          L 2   Thence

---

* Rods of Liquorice sweetly smile
In that rich Angelick Isle
          See Book 52, Stanza 48.

Veni Darlington, *servans leges*
In custodiendo greges.

Inde Middlam *cursum flecto,*
Spe lucrandi tramite recto,
Nullum renuo laborem,
Quæstus sapiens odorem;
" *Nulla via modo vera,*
" *Est ad bonos mores sera.*"

Tra-montana Fora.

Hisce foris nullum bonum
Capiens, Septentrionem
Ocyore peto pede,
Ditiore frui sede
Asperæ cautes, ardui colles,
Lucri gratia mihi molles.

Veni Appleby, *ubi natus,*
Primam sedem Comitatus.

Illinc

Thence to *Darlington*, never fwerving
From our Drove, Laws worth obferving.

Thence to *Middlam* am I aiming
In a direct courfe of gaining;
I refufe no kind of Labour,
Where I fmell fome gainful Savour:
" No way, be it ne'er the homelieft,
" Is rejected, being honeft."

Tra-montane Fairs.

In thefe Fairs, if I find nothing
Worth the ftaying, I'm no flow thing;
To the *North* frame I my Paffage,
Wing'd with Hope of more Advantage ·
Ragged Rocks, and fteepy Hillows,
Are by Gain more foft than Pillows.

Thence to Native *Appleby* mount I,
Th' ancient Seat of all that County.

L 3

Thence

Illinc Penrith *speciosam,*
Omni merce copiosam.

Illinc Roslay, *ubi tota*
Grex à gente venit Scota.

Hinc per limitem obliquam.
Veni Ravinglass *antiquam ,*
Illinc Dalton *peramœnum ,*
Hinc Oustonum *fruge plenum*
Donec Hauxide *specto sensim ;*
Illinc sedem Lancastriensem

Veni Garstang, *ubi nata*
Sunt armenta fronte latâ.

Hinc ad Ingleforth *ut descendi,*
Pulchri vituli sunt emendi.

Illinc Burton *Limina peto,*
Grege lautâ, fronde læta

Veni

Thence to Pearlefs *Penrith* went I,
Which of Merchandife hath plenty.

Thence to *Roflay*, where our Lot is
To commerce with People *Scottifh*.

By a Paffage crook'dly tending,
Thence to *Ravinglafs* I'm bending :
Thence to *Dalton*, moft delightful ;
Thenc to Oaten *Oufton* fruitful ;
Thence to *Hauxide*'s marifh Pafture ;
Thence to th' Seat of old *Lancafter*.

Thence to *Garftang*, where are feeding
Herds with large Fronts, freely breeding.

Thence to *Ingleforth* I defcended,
Where choice Bull-calfs will be vended.

Thence to *Burton*'s Bounders pafs I,
Fair in Flocks, in Paftures graffy.

L 4

Thence

Veni Horneby, *sedem claram,*
" *Spes lucrandi fert avarum;*
Cœca-sacra fames auri
Me consortem fecit Tauri.
Sprevi Veneris *amorem*
" *Lucrum summum dat odorem.*"

Veni Lonesdale, *venientem*
Laticem socii præpotentem
Haurientes, hæsitartes,
Fluctuantes, titubantes,
Allicerent, (harro verum)
Sed non sum qui semel eram.
Me ad limen trahunt Orci,
Uti lutum petunt Porci,
Aut ad vomitum fertur Canis,
Sed intentio fit inanis ·
Oculis clausis hos consortes
Præterire didici mortis.

                                   Mutil.

Thence *Horneby*, Seat renowned,
" Thus with Gain are Worldlings drowned;
Secret-facred Thirft of Treafure
Makes my Bullocks my beft Pleafure :
Should *Love* wooe me, I'd not have her,
" It is Gain yields fweeteft Savour."

Thence to *Lonefdale*, where were at it
Boys that fcorn'd Quart-Ale by Statute,
Till they ftagger'd ftammer'd ftumbled.
Railed, reeled, rouled, tumbled,
Mufing I fhould be fo 'ftranged,
I refolv'd them I was changed.
To the Sink of Sin they drew me,
Where like Hogs in Mire they threw me,
Or like Dogs unto their Vomit,
But their Purpofe I o'ercomed,
With fhut Eyes I flung in Anger
From thofe Mates of Death and Danger.

Mirtil.

Mirtil.

Miror (Fauſtule) *miror verè,*
Bacchi *te clientem heri,*
Spreto genio jucundo,
Mentem immerſiſſe Mundo :
Dic quid agis, ubi vivis,
Semper eris Mundo civis?

Fauſtul.

Errâs (Mirtille) *ſi me credas*
Nunquam Bacchi *petere ſedes ;*
Thyrſus *vinctus erit collo,*
" *Semel in anno ridet* Apollo,
Pellens animi dolores,
Mutem crines, nunquam mores.
Socios habeo verè gratos,
Oppidanus propè natos,

Intra

Mirtil.

Surely (*Fauftulus* I do wonder
How thou, who fo long liv'd under
Bacchus, where choice Wits refounded,
Shouldft be thus i'th' World drowned.
What do'ft? where liv'ft? in brief deliver.
Wilt thou be a Worldling ever?

Fauftul

Thou err'ft (*Mirtillus*) fo do mo too,
If thou think'ft I never go to
Bacchus Temple, which I follow;
" Once a Year laughs wife *Apollo*;
Where I drench Grief's flight Phyficians,
Hair I change, but no Conditions.
Cheerful Comrades have I by me,
Townfmen that do neighbour nigh me;

Within,

Intra, extra, circa muros,
Qui mordaces tollunt curas .
Hisce juvat sociari,
*Et * apricis spatiari.*

Nunc ad Richmond, *primo flore.*
Nunc ad Nesham *cum Uxore,*
Læto cursu properamus,
Et amamur & amamus ·
Pollent floribus ambulacra,
Vera Veris *simulachra.*

Nunc ad Ashton *invitato*
Ab amico & cognato,
Dant hospitium abditæ cellæ,
Radiantes Orbis Stellæ.
Mensa, mera, omnia plena,
Grata fronte & serena.

Nunc

---

* Si per apricos spatiari locos
  Gaudeat, mentem relevare meam
  Anxiam curis, studiisque gravem.

Within, without, where'er I reft me,
Carking Cares do ne'er moleft me:
With thefe I pleafe to confort me,
And in * open Fields to fport me.

Now to *Richmond*, when Spring's come on,
Now to *Nefham* with my Woman;
With free Courfe we both approve it,
Where we love, and are beloved;
Here Fields flower with frefheft Creatures,
Reprefenting *Flora*'s Features.

Now to *Afhton*, I'm invited
By my Friend and Kinfman cited;
Secret Cellars entertain me.
Beauteous-beaming Stars inflame me;
Meat, Mirth, Mufick Wines are there full,
With a Count'nance blith and cheerful.

Now

---

* Thus thro' the fair Fields, when I have beft }
      Leifure, }
   Diaper'd richly, do I take my Pleafure. }
   To cheer my Studies with a Pleafing Meafure. }

Nunc ad Cowbrow, *ubi lætus,*
Una mente confluit cœtus,
Nescit locus lachrymare,
Nescit hospes osculari,
Facit in amoris testem
Anser vel Gallina festum.

Nunc ad Natland, *ubi* Florem
Convivalem & Pastorem
Specto, spiro ora rosea,
A queis Nectar *&* Ambrosia
Castitatis autem curæ
Me intactum servant rure.

Nunc ad Kirkland, *& de eo*
" Prope Templo, procul Deo,"
Dici potest, spectent Templum,
Sacerdotis & exemplum,
Audiant tamen citius sonum
Tibiæ tamen concionem.

Nunc

Now to *Cowbrow*, quickly thither
Jovial Boys do flock together ;
In which place all Sorrow loft is,
Guefts know how to kifs their Hoftefs ;
Nought but Love doth border near it.
Goofe and Hen will witnefs bear it.

Now to *Natland*, where choice Beauty
And a Shepherd do falute me ;
Lips I Relifh richly Rofeack,
Purely *Nectar* and *Ambrofiack* ;
But I'm chafte, as doth become me,
For the Country's Eyes are on me.

Now to *Kirkland*, truly by it
May that Say' be verified,
" *Far from G O D, but near the Temple,*
Tho' their Paftor gave Example :
They are fuch a kind of Vermin,
Pipe they'd rather hear than Sermon.

Nunc ad Kendal, *propter* * *Pannum,*
Cœtum, situm, † Aldermannum,
Virgines pulchras, pias matres,
Et viginti quatuor fratres,
Verè clarum & beatum,
Mihi nactum, notum, natum.
Ubi dicam (pace vestra)
Tectum mittitur è fenestra,
Cura lucri, cura fori,
Saltant cum Johanne Dori
Sancti fratres cum Poeta,
Læta canunt & faceta.

Nunc ad Staveley, *ubi aves*
Melos, modos cantant suaves,

Sub

---

* Lanificii gloria, & industri ita præcellens,
ut eo nomine sit celeberrimum   *Camd* Brit
Pannus mihi Panis.   *Mot.*

† Nomine *Major* eas, nec sis minor omine sedis,
Competat ut titulo civica Vita novo

Now to *Kendal*, for * Cloth-making,
Sight, fite, † Alderman awaking;
Beauteous Damfels, modeft Mothers,
And her four and twenty Brothers;
Ever in her Honour fpreading,
Where I had my Native Breeding.
Where, I'll tell you, (while none mind us)
We threw th' Houfe quite out at Windows;
Nought maketh them or me ought forry,
They dance lively with *John Dory*
Holy Brethren with their Poet
Sing, nor care they much who know it.

Now to *Staveley* ftrait repair I,
Where fweet Birds do hatch, their airy
M   Arbours,

---

* A Town fo highly renown'd for her commo-
dious Clothing, and induftrious Trading, as her
Name is become famous in that kind. *Camb Brit.*
Cloth is my Bread.   *Motto*

† Now haft thou chang'd thy Title unto May'r,
Let Life, State, Style, improve thy Charter there

Sub arbuſtis & virgultis
Molliore maſco fultis ·
Cellis, Sylvis, & Tabernis,
An fœliciorem cernis?

Mirtil.

E*STO* Fauſtule' *recumbe,*
    Rure tuo carmina funde;
Vive, vale, proſice, creſce,
Arethuſæ *alma meſſe ,*
Tibi Zephyrus *ſub fago*
Dulciter afflet.   Fauſt.] G*ratias ago.*

AD

Arbours, Oziers freſhly ſhowing,
With ſoft moſſy Rhind o'er growing.
For Woods, Air, A L E, all excelling:
Wouldſt thou have a neater Dwelling?

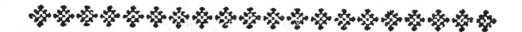

Myrtil.

BE't ſo, *Fauſtulus* ! there repoſe thee,
Cheer thy Country with thy Poeſy;
Live, fare well, as thou deſerveſt,
Rich in *Arethuſa*'s Harveſt
Under th' Beach while Shepherds rank thee
Zephyrus bleſs thee.   *Fauſt*] I do thank thee.

AD
PHILOXENUM.

T E *Viatores lepidi Patronum,*
Te tuæ dicunt patriæ coronam,
Vatis & vitis roseæ corymbum,
Artis alumum.

Te tuus Vates Lyricis salutat
Qui fidem nulla novitate mutat,
Nec nova venti levitate nutat,
Fidus ad aras.

TO

TO
PHILOXENUS.

THE pleaſing Waymates titled have their
    Patron,
Their Country's Glory, which they build their
    State on,
The Poet's Wine-buſh, which they uſe to
    prate on,
        Art's merry Minion.

In Lyrick Meaſures doth they Bard ſalute thee,
Who with a conſtant Reſolution ſuits thee,
Nor can ought move me to remove me from
    thee,
       But my Religion.

Efficit egregios nobilis alla viros.

Fœcundi calices quem non fecere difertum?

Inflatum hesterno venas, ut semper, Iaccho,

*Si vitulum spectes, nihil est quod pocula
laudes.*

BESSIE

The Oil of Malt, and Juice of fpritely Nectar
Have made my Mufe more valiant than *Hector*.

O'erflowing Cups, whom have they not made
 learned ?

Full-blown my Veins are, and fo well they
 may,
With brimming Healths of Wine drunk yefter-
 day.

If thou doft love thy Flock, leave off to Pot.

BESSIE BELL:

Cantio Latinè Verſa, alternis Vicibus & modernis Vocibus decantanda.

Authore *Corymbæo*.

Damætas.   **Eliza-Bella.**

I.

Dam. BEllula Bella, *mi puella,*
　　　　Tu me corde tenes,
O ſi clauſa ſimus cella
Mars & Lemnia Venus!

　　　　　　　　　　　Tanto

BESSY BELL:

To be ſung in altern Courſes and modern Voices.

By Corymbæus.

Damætas.   Eliza-Bella.

I.

Dam.   MY bonny *Bell*, I love thee ſo well,
        I would thou wad ſcund alang
              hither,

That we might here in a Cellar dwell,
And blend our Bows together !

                              Dear

Tanto mi es, quanti tua res,
Ne fpectes Bellala Mundum,
Non locus eft cui crimen obeft
In amoribus ad cocundum.

II.

Bel. *Crede Damætas, non finit ætas*
Ferre Cupidinis ignem,
Vir verè lætus intende pecus
Cura & Carmine dignum.
Non amo te, ne tu ames me,
Nam jugo premitur gravi,
Quæcunque nubit & uno cubat,
Nec amo, nec amor, nec amavi.

III.

Dam. *Virginis vita fit inimica*
Principi, patriæ, proli,
In Orbe fita ne fis invita
Sponfa nitidula coli.

Afpice

Dear art' to me as thy Geer's to thee,
The World will never ſuſpect us,
This Place it is private, 'tis Folly to drive it,
Love's Spies have no Eyes to detect us.

II.

Bell. Truſt me, *Damætas*, Youth will not let us
Yet to be ſindg'd with Love's Taper,
Bonny blith Swainlin intend thy Lambkin,
To requ te both thy Laws and thy Labour.
I love not thee, why ſhould'ſt thou love me?
The Yoke I cannot approve it,
Then lie ſtill with one, I'd rather have none,
Nor I love, nor am lov'd, nor have loved.

III.

Dam. To lead Apes in Hell, it will not do well,
'Tis an Enemy to Procreation,
In the World to tarry, and never to marry,
Would bring it ſoon to Deſolation.

See

Aſpice vultum numine cultum,
Flore, colore jucundum,
Hic locus eſt, nam lucus adeſt
In amoribus ad coeundum.

IV.

Bel. *Ah pudet fari, cogor amari,*
Volo, ſed nolo fateri,
Expedit mari lenocinari,
At libet iſta tacere.
Non amo te, quid tu amas me?
Nam jugo premitur gravi
Quæcunque nubit & uno cubat,
Nec amo, nec amor, nec amavi.

V.

Dam. *Candida Bella, ſplendida Stella,*
Languida lumina cerne,
Emitte mella Eliz-Bella,
Lentula tædia ſperne.

Mors

See my count'nance merry, cheeks red as Cherry
This Cover will never ſuſpect us,
This Place it is private, 'tis Folly to drive it,
Love's Spies have no Eyes to detect us.

IV.

Bell. 'Las Maidens muſt feign it, I love, tho'
     I lain it,
I would, but I will not confeſs it,
My Years are conſorting, and fain would be
     ſporting,
But Baſhfulneſs ſhames to expreſs it.
I love not thee, why ſhouldſt thou love me ?
That Yoke I cannot approve it,
Then lie ſtill with one, I'd rather have none,
Nor I love, nor am lov'd, nor have loved.

V.

Dam. My beauteous *Bell,* who Stars do excel,
See mine Eyes never drys, but do wet me,
Some comfort unbuckle, my ſweet Honyſuckle,
Come away, do not ſtay, I entreat thee.
                     Delay

Mors mihi mora, hac ipsâ horâ
Jungamus ora per undam,
Nam locus eſt cui crimen abeſt
In amoribus ad coeundum

VI.

Bel.   *Perge* Damætas, *nunc pruriit ætas,*
Me nudam accipe ſolam,
Demitte pecus ſi Bellam *petas,*
Exue virginis ſtolam.
Sic amo te, ſi tu ames me,
Nam jugo premitur ſuavi,
Quæcunque nubit & uno cubat,
Et amo, & amor, & amavi.

F I N I S.

Delay would undo me, hie quickly unto me,
This River will never ſuſpect us,
This Place it is private, 'tis Folly to drive it,
Love's Spies have no Eyes to detect us.

VI.

Bell. Come on, *Damœtas*, ripe Age doth fit us,
Take aſide thy nak'd Bride, and enjoy her,
So thou cull thy Sweeting, let Flocks fall a
    bleating,
My Maids Weed on thy Mede I'll beſtow there.
Thus I love thee, ſo do thou love me,
The Yoke is ſo ſweet, I approve it,
To lie ſtill with one, is better than none,
I do love, I am lov'd, and have lov'd it.

The E N D.

A N

I N D E X

O F T H E

Men, Places, Signs, &c.

A

A Berford   *Page* 19
     Aldermanbury, *at the* Axe, *p.* 61
Alerton   113, 147
Appleby   149
Aſhton   39, 157
Aſk. 'g   123
Author marries, and turns Farmer   145
Addreſs to Philoxenus   164

B

Bainbrig   123
Banbury   5

Ba-

INDEX.

Banister, *a noted Inkeeper at* Preston, 39
Barnet, *at the* Purse, *the Bears made him
    bewray himself*   59
Bautree   101
Bessy Bell, *a Song*   169
Bradford   23
Bramham   107
Brickhill   55
Bruarton, *a merry Story*   47
Budworth, *at the* Cock   43
Buntingford   79
Burleigh   91
Burton   151
Brackley   9

C

Cambridge   81
Cardinal's Hat   63
Carperby   119
Caxston   79
Clapham   25
Clowne   17
Coleshill, *the Butcher's Wife there,*   49
Coventry, *for Blue*   51
Cowbrow   27, 159
Cranes (Three)   63

D

Daventree   51
Dalton   151

Dar-

I N D E X.

Darlington 117, 149
Doncafter 17, 101
Dunchurch 51
Dunftable 57
Dory (John) *danc'd with* 161

E

Eufton 41

F

Ferrybrig 103

G

Gandy (Tom) 43
Garftang 39, 151
Gaftile 125
Gigglefwick 23
Godmanchefter 81
Godftow 7
Gottham 11
Green (Franc.) *of* Stratfoid, *and his handfome Wife* 55
Griffin *in the* Old-Baily 63
Grantham 95

H

Hardraw 123
Harrington 83
Harts-horns 63
Hauxide 151
Haywood 47
Helperby 111

High-

INDEX.

High-gate, *the Horn there*   59
Hockly-hole   55
Hoddefden   75
Holbourn-bridge, *at the* Rofe   63
Holloway   61
Holm-Chapel, *for Ale*   43
Hornby   153
Huntington   83

I

Ingleforth   151
Ingleton   25
John   (Little)   13
John à Gaunt   37
Iflington, *at the* Lyon   61, 73

K

Kendal   127, 161
Kighley   23
Killington   127
Kingfland   73
Kirkland   29, 59
Knaves-acre *near* York, *where the Piper was hang'd, and play'd afterwards,* 109

L

Leicefter, *at the* Bell   9
Leave taken of all the Places he drank at, from p. 135 *to* p. 145

Litch-

INDEX.

Litchfield, *he borrow'd Money of an Old Usurer*   49
London   73
Lonesdale   27, 153
Lousy-Hill   115

M

Maidenly John   123
Malton   145
Mansfield   13
Meredin, *merry with his Landlady* Joan, 49
Middlam   119, 149
Mother Red-Cap's *at* Holloway   59

N

Natland   27, 159
Nesham, *for its Nunnery famous*   115
Newcastle Under-line   45
Newfound College   87
Newton *in the Willows*   41
Newark   97
Nottingham   11

O

Overbowles   13
Ouston   151
Oxford   7

P

Penrith   151
Pomfret. *for Liquorice*   147
Preston   39

Puc-

INDEX

Puckeridge 77

R

Rainesford, *the Prelate there* 82
Ravinglaſs 151
Redbourn 57
Redmeer 117
Retford 99
Richmond 117, 157
Ridgelay 47
Rippon 145
Robin Hood, *p.* 13.   *His Well.* p. 103
Roſamond's *Bower* 7
Roſe, *a pretty Girl at* Newton *in* Lanca-
   ſhire 45
Roſlay 151
Rothram, *at the* Bull 17
Royſton 79

S

Sarah's Hole 93
Sautry 85
Scarlet, Robin Hood's *Man* 13
Scrubie 99
Sedbergh 125
Sherbuin 105
Sherwood 11
Smeton 115
St. Albans 59

Stam-

I N D E X.

Stamford	93
Staveley	29, 61
Stilton	87
Stone, *at the* Bell	45
Stonegate-hole	83
Stratford	55

T

Tadcaster	107
Tauk-a-Hill	45
Theobalds	73
Thyrsk	113, 147
Topcliff	111, 147
Toceter, *where he sate up all Night,*	53
Totnam Highcross	73

W

Wademill	77
Wakefield *Pindar*	21
Waltham-Abbey	75
Wansforth-brigs	89
Ware	77
Warrington	43
Wedon, *where he vomited*	53
Wentbridge	103
Wenchly	19
Wetherbe	21
Wigan	41
Witham	95

Wood-

INDEX.

Woodstock   7

Worton   121

Y

York, *where he lay with the Weaver's Wife*   107

Young, *the Tobacconist*   65

Younger (Tom) *of* Brickhill   55

CPSIA information can be obtained
at www.ICGtesting.com
Printed in the USA
BVHW022242291222
655301BV00006B/146